Praise for WHO HATES WHOM *by Bob Harris*

"Bob Harris, perpetual *Jeopardy!* underdog, now turns his polymathic curiosity to the subject of GLOBAL CONFLICT—the result: this handy history of violence that is at once surprising, fascinating, enlightening, and surprisingly NOT TOTALLY DEPRESSING. A gimlet-eyed look at the world we endure that's also suitable for enjoying with a gimlet."
—**John Hodgman**, author of *The Areas of My Expertise* and correspondent for *The Daily Show with Jon Stewart*

"The geopolitical equivalent of scorecards that get hawked at ball games. Only Bob could make a user's guide to our increasingly hostile world this absorbing, this breezy, and—ultimately—this hopeful."
—**Ken Jennings**, author of *Brainiac: Adventures in the Curious, Competitive, Compulsive World of Trivia Buffs*

"It takes a deft touch to combine this much-needed research with a razor-sharp wit. . . . You'll laugh 'til you cry, but at least you'll be one step ahead of CNN."
—**Gus Russo**, author of *Supermob* and *The Outfit*

"If you read one book this year, be like me and choose this one."
—**Emo Philips**

Also by Bob Harris

Prisoner of Trebekistan: A Decade in Jeopardy!

WHO
HATES
WHOM

WELL-ARMED FANATICS, INTRACTABLE CONFLICTS, AND VARIOUS THINGS BLOWING UP

A Woefully Incomplete Guide

BOB HARRIS

THREE RIVERS PRESS
NEW YORK

DEDICATION

To the countless millions of

innocent human beings

who have died

because other human beings

were certain

they were doing the right thing

Library of Congress Cataloging-in-Publication Data

Harris, Bob, 1963–
Who hates whom : well-armed fanatics, intractable conflicts, and various
things blowing up : a woefully incomplete guide / Bob Harris.—1st ed.
         p. cm.
   1. History—Miscellanea.   2. Curiosities and wonders.   3. Social
conflict.   4. Interpersonal conflict.   5. Ethnic conflict.   I. Title
                         D10.H25 2007
303.6—dc22   2007017846

ISBN 978-0-307-39436-1

Printed in the United States of America

Design by Lenny Henderson

10 9 8 7 6 5

First Edition

CONTENTS

CONTENTS

INTRODUCTION/FOREWORD THINGY

Visiting a museum in Turkey, I once stumbled across the oldest surviving peace treaty, inscribed in clay more than three thousand years ago. After history's greatest chariot battle, the Egyptians and Hittites reached the agreement pictured at right:

These shreds of clay—the Treaty of Kadesh—defined the border between two vast empires in terms that allowed both sides to claim victory. The treaty, therefore, promised "good peace" throughout the entire region. "Forever."

And here's a map of that region today:

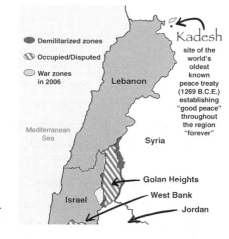

Yikes.

1

Three thousand years later—October 2006—I was in my editor's office, batting around ideas for my next book. However, my favorite notion—a chronicle of weird sports worldwide—didn't grab him. (The only sport that *really* sells books is golf. You could do a coffee table book of Tiger Woods organizing his attic, and it would sell.) It was late, so we gave up.

I didn't mind. I love to travel, so I figured I'd get on some planes, revisit Trebekistan, and stumble across an idea. Unfortunately, lots of places I want to visit—Victoria Falls, say, or Persepolis, Cartagena, or the Chocolate Hills of Bohol—seem permanently surrounded by turbulence. So on our way out, I wished for a book to exist—entitled, I dunno, *Who Hates Whom,* maybe—with little essays and maps that would help me understand in simple terms which parts of the planet are currently explosive and why.

"That's not bad, actually," my editor said. "You want to write it?"

In a lunatic moment of hubris, I said yes. So this is that. My best shot, anyway. But had my editor been in a more whimsical mood, this book might have been about Malaysian foot volleyball, German chessboxing, and Turkish camel wrestling.

So, the ground rules:

- This book is meant to be handy when you see something explode on CNN but they switch to Anna Nicole Smith still being dead before you're sure what went kaboom. So we're looking mostly at Third World powder kegs, although since many conflicts remain rooted in colonial decisions, a few former colonial powers get entries, too.

  A more accurate title might have been *Who's Currently Blowing Up Whom, or Did Recently, or Is Probably About To,* but the cover isn't big enough, and too many people might miss the fourth word.

- In no way is this comprehensive. I omitted the United States, for example, since this edition is mostly for U.S. readers, and you already know whom you've recently hated and feared. There should probably be more here about Russia and China, but they deserve whole books, and in the space allotted I wanted to give you a variety pack. There's nothing here about Senegal's civil war, Fiji's recent coup, or a dozen other significant conflicts. If your favorite insurrection or oppressive power didn't make the cut, my bad.

- Obviously, these essays aren't up to the minute. Writing a book about ongoing battles is like doing an oil painting of a fireworks display. I can try to fill in the history and context and players, but for updates, you're on your own.

- I claim no expertise. Zero. My degree is in electrical engineering, and I've been a comic, a TV writer, a memoirist, a TV debunker of urban legends, and the voice of a cartoon penguin, all of which qualifies me for squat. I'm lucky I'm allowed to drive. While everything should be pretty easy to verify from reputable sources in two Googles, surely there are errors I haven't caught. I eagerly await being told of each one five minutes after publication. See WhoHatesWhom.com for errata and notes.

- Don't worry if you've never heard of Baluchistan and the like. I certainly hadn't until working on this. If it helps, I'm friends with Ken Jennings and Brad Rutter, the two biggest winners in the history of *Jeopardy!*, and they hadn't heard of Baluchistan, either. And they know how many fingers you're holding up right now.

- I have come to recommend strongly against looking for "good guys." Conflicts often aren't two-sided, and our capacity for rationalization means even the "right" side usually does lousy things. So be ready for conflicts with two marginally bad guys, three bad guys and no good guys, etc.

• I made the graphics myself in Photoshop, based on public domain data, news reports, and government resources. (I took all the pictures, too.) Map boundaries may be off by a smidge. Please don't spaz. Political boundaries are fictional and temporary anyhow. No insult ever intended to your particular shade of gray.

Incidentally, maps are inherently filled with political choices. In a civil war, which city is the capital? (I just show every relevant city.) If a boundary is disputed, where do you draw the line? (The UN has handy suggestions.) What about disputed territories with multiple names? (Most common usage wins.) Common usage rules country names, too: Egypt is *Egypt,* not *Misr;* India is *India,* not *Bharat;* etc. But Ivory Coast is *Côte d'Ivoire,* because they've been asking nicely for decades.

Acronyms are in original languages: the French group Médecins Sans Frontières (Doctors Without Borders) would be abbreviated MSF here, not DWB.

• I avoid the word *terrorism,* for moral and clarity reasons. For one, its common usage—violence against civilians by non-state actors as an absolute evil—subtly implies that officially sanctioned carnage is somehow more legit. *Eek.* Whether an air force blows up your village or rebels bomb it from ground level, the objectives and results are the same. (The UN definition makes no distinction between state and non-state terror, but popular usage does. No wonder governments like the word.)

Terrorist is also distorted simply to mean "enemy." Nepalese Maoists were "terrorists" right up until they helped abolish an abusive monarchy. They're now the prime minister's cabinet during a peaceful transition to democracy. While Nelson Mandela was fighting apartheid, the White House deemed his party "terrorist," but an anti-Castro militant accused of involvement in killing seventy-three civilians on a Cuban airliner went to work for Oliver North. And when rebels in Sierra Leone were hacking off people's arms *specifically in order to terrify people,* the word was rarely even suggested, although you couldn't ask for a more precise example. Even Amnesty International used *terrorism* to refer only to Al-Qaeda, which may have benefited from the blood diamond trade.

Worse, the word obliterates distinctions. "Terrorists" in Lebanon, Sri Lanka, Spain, and Peru almost sound like they're teammates, but they have literally nothing in common. Tossing complex, violent agendas into a giant bin called terrorism is both lazy and dangerous. Instead, let's force ourselves to use specifics: "nationalist rebels" or "drug-financed paramilitary death squads" or "sex-crazed vegetarian pacifists." Speaking of which, not enough sex-crazed vegetarian pacifists are invading people. I checked.

Everyone knows how horrible 9-11 was. We don't minimize it by refusing to use a meaningless word. Instead, we force ourselves to think. This may be a useful habit.

• If you're a well-armed paramilitary cell, a separatist group liberating your minority, or a religious movement purifying society, and you think I've described your blowing-up-of-stuff unfairly, please consider: I am a reasonable man. More important, I am also spineless. Simply contact me via the publisher, explain how I've misrepresented your cause, and with luck I will happily apologize, try to include your side of things more fairly in the next edition, and continue to enjoy full use of my physical body.

- My own biases and agenda: I was born in 1963, so my childhood came when the U.S. civil rights, women's equality, and peace movements were just being co-opted by mass commercialism. When I was a boy watching TV, herds of people of every color sang together atop a mountain; global harmony was just a gulp of sugar water away. Surely peace and equality were at hand. Maybe it's my Sunday school upbringing, or an emotional need to believe in *something* now that I'm too old for Sunday school. Whichever. The idea that peace *is* possible, despite a few thousand years of human history arguing otherwise, is still hard-wired in my head. Whether that's foolish or noble or just well programmed is your call, not mine. But there it is.

- I've also lived most of my life in the United States—and for all its faults, the U.S. is history's best example of a country where people from literally the entire planet manage to live in peace, all at once. In Los Angeles or New York, as in the world's other great cities, you interact constantly with people whose ancestors came from almost every corner of the globe. If you notice, the possibility of a peaceful world is stunningly self-evident.

So I still have hope. Even after writing the book that follows. More now, in fact.

This may be the last political thing I write for a very long time; this project has reinforced the *Trebekistan* realization that I know so incredibly little. Maybe I'd rather keep my own yap shut for a while. There is much to learn.

But getting a thumbnail feel for once-mysterious conflicts also removes a lot of fear from the world. None of our wars are truly incomprehensible, and all of them seem to arise from basic stuff any of us can understand. And when we human beings understand one another, we seem to kill one another a lot less.

Ironically, then, this is a very hopeful book. What I ultimately hope to offer here is a sense of shared humanity, even at our most horrible.

That's probably when we need it most.

MIDDLE EAST/
CENTRAL ASIA

AFGHANISTAN/PAKISTAN

- Mujahedin (Pashtuns, other local factions, and foreign fighters) v. Soviets (defunct)
- Taliban (Pashtuns) v. other local factions (pre-9-11)
- Waziris v. Pakistan (treaty, 2006)
- Taliban (Pashtuns), Al-Qaeda (foreign fighters), and some Waziris v. U.S., NATO, and some Waziris, ongoing

To make sense here at all, let's walk through this one step at a time.

THE PASHTUNS

 orders drawn along ethnic or cultural lines don't necessarily equate with peace—compare the homogenous Korean peninsula to multilingual Canada, for example—but cultural loyalties trump colonial boundaries every time. So here's how the British drew the 1893 Durand Line through the Pashtuns, the dominant people of the border area:

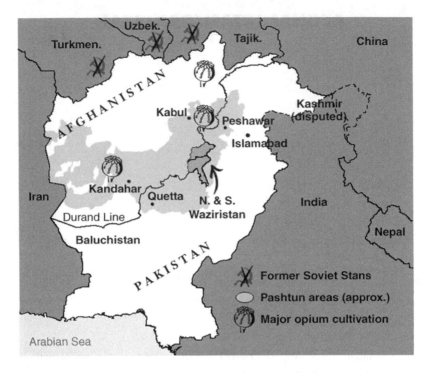

Why all the divide and conquer? The British had a vast empire to the southeast, including modern Pakistan, India, Bangladesh, Myanmar, and Sri Lanka.* Worried about Russia to the north, the British spent the 19th century trying to set up Afghanistan as a buffer zone, yet without empowering the Pashtuns enough to create yet another threat. Thus the Durand Line.

However, the Pashtuns had once ruled much of this whole region themselves, and they've been here for centuries. Alexander the Great (for whom Kandahar is named), Persians, Arabs, Mongols, Mughals,

---

*Note that Afghanistan, Pakistan, India, Bangladesh, Myanmar, and Sri Lanka were all obvious choices for this book. The struggles of former colonies with arbitrary boundaries and other colonial aftereffects are a common source of war.

Brits, and Soviets have each rolled through, but Peshawar and Kandahar have nonetheless remained firmly Pashtun. (Pashtun survival stems in part from *Pashtunwali*, a complex two-thousand-year-old code of honor. Grossly oversimplified: befriend a Pashtun and he will die for you. Piss off a Pashtun, and his neighbor's great-grandchildren may hate yours.) Not surprisingly, in 1949, a Pashtun *loya jirga* (a tribal council, like the end of *Survivor* with longer beards) denounced the Durand Line, which has been ignored in some areas all along. Point being: in some areas, the border is porous to nonexistent.

So you can't really discuss Afghanistan and Pakistan as separate deals, at least not near the border. They aren't.

THE MUJAHEDIN, AL-QAEDA, AND THE TALIBAN

"The enemy of my enemy is my friend" may work on playgrounds, but the enemy of your enemy can be *your* enemy, too. This will be good to keep in mind.

In 1979, the Soviets invaded Afghanistan to support their puppet government, which tortured and killed thousands. Seizing a chance to weaken their enemy, the U.S. armed Islamist mujahedin ("holy warriors"; notice the word *jihad* in the middle), Pakistan provided training, and Saudi Arabia financed religious schools (madrasahs) to use extreme Islamist ideology as a recruiting tool against communism. (Pursuit of Islamic governance—whether by violent or nonviolent means—is described as "Islamist" as opposed to garden-variety "Islamic," which just refers to the religion in general. Two letters, big difference.)

This worked too well, creating a generation of radicals who saw enemies of their freshly brewed puritanical Islam not just among communists, but everywhere—including the U.S., Pakistan, and Saudi Arabia. Whoops.

In the 1980s, a Saudi trust-fund kid moved to Peshawar, using family money to bring fighters worldwide into the madrasahs and

Afghanistan. This was Osama Bin Laden; Al-Qaeda ("the base") refers either to a specific camp or a database of foreign fighters (sources disagree). Bin Laden eventually split from his mujahedin allies, focused his hatred on the Saudi government for allowing U.S. bases on Saudi soil, and wound up exiled to Sudan for a while (see "Sudan," page 64). After the Soviet defeat in Afghanistan, various factions (several funded by opium) fought over the pieces. Pakistan still had an unstable neighbor, and the mujahedin still didn't have their Islamist state. Making common cause, Pakistani intelligence organized a Pashtun faction of madrasah-trained Taliban ("students" in Pashto) to stabilize Afghanistan. (*Stabilize* here means "invade and oppress.")

Pakistan hoped that by holding the purse strings of extremists like Mullah Mohammad Omar, they could keep a lid on things. However, while not all Pashtun are Taliban, virtually all Taliban are Pashtun. And Pashtunwali means that many non-Taliban Pashtuns—plus Waziris and other related Pashto speakers—will favor the Taliban over non-Pashtuns. So this was a recipe for spreading extremism.

In 1996, the Taliban captured Kabul, hunted down the last Soviet ruler, ripped off his testicles, shot him, and hung his body from a streetlamp. Then they got nasty.

For obvious reasons, the Taliban were recognized as a government only by Pakistan, Saudi Arabia, and the Saudi-influenced United Arab Emirates. But soon Osama Bin Laden returned from Sudan, settled into Kandahar, married one of his sons to Mullah Omar's daughter, and started funding and providing personnel to the Taliban. In turn the Taliban let Osama and his motley foreign Islamists hang out.

EXTREMIST BELIEFS
Taliban consider themselves pure traditional Muslims, but their ideology is influenced by the relatively recent works of an Egyptian

named Sayyid Qutb, whose writings from prison in the 1950s and 1960s are like a bizarro *Letters from a Birmingham Jail,* replacing Dr. King's nonviolence and compassion with violent contempt for most of humanity.

Qutb's world was utterly simplistic: to him, Islam was already dead, having wandered far from its pure, narrow path. A few remnants fit into Qutb's harsh version of Islamic law, but everything else was inherently evil and corrupt. Therefore, for Qutb, the non-Islamic world—including not just the West, but the vast majority of mainstream Muslims and all secular governments, especially in Muslim countries—was the enemy.

"You're either with us or against us," in other words.

Egypt hanged Qutb in 1966, but his works continue to provide deceptively simple, emotionally satisfying answers to complex social questions. Followers, including Osama's pal Ayman al-Zahawiri, have amplified his ideas, building the case to abolish all democracies and even nationalities. Instead: a worldwide Taliban-plus, forever.

But be reassured: Qutb is considered a heretic by most mainstream Muslims. The notion that the Koran can be so radically interpreted is usually seen as a serious insult to 1,300 years of tradition. And despite wide disdain for U.S. policies amplified during the Bush years, only a small bit of the Islamic world identifies with this stuff, and only a teeny percentage of *those* would engage in any violence. Even the Egyptian Muslim Brotherhood, Qutb's home team, has moved away from his rhetoric in recent years.

In short, most of the world's hundreds of millions of Muslims are *not* part of an extremist offshoot that seeks their own destruction. The West can either earnestly pursue relationships with moderate Muslims in difficult countries, or simply slur them all together as enemies, a move as sloppy and hostile as it is self-fulfilling.

THE TERROR AND DRUG WARS
AT CROSS-PURPOSES

When not attacking civilization, harboring Bin Laden, and oppressing women, the Taliban also eradicated opium. (Supposedly this was out of Islamist fervor, but they're dealing in it now, so this looks more like it was a consolidation of power: opium was a possible source of financing for rivals.)

As part of the U.S. drug war, the Bush administration rewarded the Taliban with $43 million in May 2001. This looked amazingly bad at the time, but went off the charts four months later. After 9-11, the West aggressively allied with the Taliban's opposition, the mostly non–Pashtun Northern Alliance, who were in opium to their eyeballs. *Whatever,* said the Pentagon, and by December 2001, the Taliban were in the hills, where the guerrilla war continues. Meanwhile, Afghanistan now produces about 90 percent of the world's opium, financing both sides.

Some big drug players in NATO-controlled areas are also potential military leaders, so arresting them hurts the alliance. Outside NATO control, the opium money often winds up in Taliban hands, which are currently making AK-47s the most popular fashion accessories in Waziristan.

WAZIRISTAN

Don't expect to thumb through *Lonely Planet Waziristan* anytime soon. While the region is ostensibly under Pakistan's rule, Waziris, kin to the Pashtuns, have lived in these mountains, unconquered, for at least six centuries.

After 9-11, Pakistan's military tried to limit Taliban movements in Waziristan. This failed; instead, Pakistan just pissed off the Waziris (remember Pashtunwali), who started killing Pakistani informants and even their own tribal leaders suspected of pro–Pakistan sympathies. Seven hundred dead Pakistanis later, in September 2006, Pakistan backed off, agreeing to let both North and South Waziristan run their own affairs. This largely just reflected existing reality.

In simple terms: on the Pakistan side of the 1893 Durand Line, the Taliban now have a quiet place to clean their guns and eat soup, returning to the Afghanistan side to fight as they choose. In response to NATO complaints, Pakistan recently began building—what else?—a fence on the border. Few observers expect this to help (see "Mexico," p. 56).

The West has few choices here. Indiscriminate bombing or high-casualty ground operations would create even more enemies, even if they had Pakistan's permission. So for now the West plays defense, watches from satellites, and lobs in the occasional Hellfire missile, while Al-Qaeda and the Taliban expand their influence, install *Sharia* law, sing the praises of suicide bombing, and generally illegalize fun.

It's still possible that Al-Qaeda, the Taliban, and the Waziris will fuss with one another; after all, Al-Qaeda and the muj once split, and fanatics do tend to piss one another off. Waziris are reportedly fighting their guests-cum-oppressors already. But this region could dearly use much of the support and focus currently diverted into Iraq, and ongoing civilian casualties have led to growing local resentment of NATO operations. If history is any guide—and it has that rude habit—the Western alliance may not leave soon with democracy in their wake.

OTHER CONFLICTS, FUTURE PROSPECTS

There's enough here for another book. In resource-rich Baluchistan, nationalists are blowing up gas pipelines, demanding a share of the profits. While relations with India are calm for now, Pakistani intelligence is frequently accused of supporting numerous anti-Indian separatist groups. Kashmir is a frequent stress, which gets its own section later (see "Kashmir," p. 106).

In 1999, Gen. Pervez Musharraf, head of Pakistan's armed forces, seized power in a widely condemned coup. Musharraf initially supported the Taliban, but after 9-11, caught between a regional power and a superpower, Musharraf rolled with the big boys. However, Pakistan's people range from Westernized technocrats of the 21st century to rural tribesmen still living in the 14th, and Musharraf's dictatorial tendencies tend to alienate the former. To retain power, he is often forced to appeal to Pashtuns and other conservatives. After two assassination attempts traced to Waziristan, Musharraf insists there's a clear split between the Taliban ("good guys" to many Pashtuns) and Al-Qaeda's assortment of Uzbeks, Tajiks, Arabs, Chechens, and other foreign fighters.

As Taliban attacks and influence spread, the stability of Pakistan's government may depend on that wish becoming true.

IRAQ

They're in the area around Tikrit and Baghdad and
east, west, south, and north somewhat.
—DONALD RUMSFELD, SPECIFYING THE
LOCATION OF WMDs AS ANYWHERE
AND STILL BEING WRONG, 2003

There is no military solution to
a problem like that in Iraq.
—GEN. DAVID PETRAEUS, COMMANDER OF U.S.
FORCES IN IRAQ, 2007

- Various insurgents v. U.S.-led alliance (guerrilla war)
- Sunni v. Shi'a (centered in Baghdad; the "civil war")
- U.S. and Kurds v. Ansar al-Islam (early in war)
- "Al-Qaeda in Iraq" v. U.S. (starting months after the invasion)
- Al-Qaeda v. Shi'a (beginning September 2005)

You've surely read that U.S. troops often aren't sure how individual missions relate to larger objectives. The map here—itself an obvious oversimplification—shows why.

The WWII invasion of Normandy was comparatively simple: (a) go get the bad guys; (b) over there. In Iraq, nothing is quite so clear.

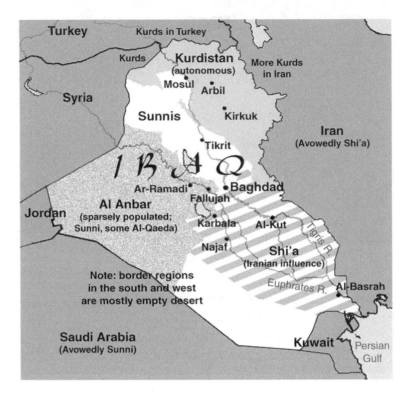

First, a few sad notes about the war's origins: Iraq had nothing resembling the WMD program the White House alleged, and Saddam
had nothing to do with 9-11. There was never any solid evidence of
either, despite the televised drumbeat for war. Osama Bin Laden's disdain for the secular dictatorship of Saddam Hussein was well known
(see "Afghanistan/Pakistan," p. 11). As to the WMDs, the former chief
UN inspector in Iraq insisted that Iraq had been essentially disarmed in
1991, and that constant U.S. satellite and aerial surveillance ever since
had produced nothing resembling a WMD program.

What *did* exist was an outside-normal-channels Office of Special
Plans (OSP) created by Donald Rumsfeld and Dick Cheney to

cherry-pick slivers of raw intelligence in order to build the case for war. (This, too, was information made public *before* the war, thanks to Air Force Lt. Col. Karen Kwiatkowski and retired Army Col. David Hackworth, who spread the word as best they could.) The Bush administration then hyped OSP's baseless tales of impending nuclear doom just prior to the 2002 midterm elections, later inserting a blatant falsehood into the 2003 State of the Union address. British government memos plainly confirm that the war decision was not based on actual intelligence—instead, the "facts were being fixed around the policy."

So what happens when a government isn't interested in facts? Iraq.

This isn't a partisan issue; Democrats and Republicans were equally gung ho, despite military tactics that fly in the face of established doctrine. (A successful invasion/occupation, for example, would normally require at least three times as many troops.)

Finally, yes, Saddam *was* blue throbbing scum, but if you haven't seen it, Google up the famous 1983 photo (which I'm too cheap to pay for) of Donald Rumsfeld happily shaking Saddam's hand, working to improve U.S./Iraqi relations—a year *after* the Dujail massacre for which Saddam was later executed.

Shortly after Don and Saddam played Hands Across Mesopotamia, U.S. aid to Iraq became a staple of the 1980s. After the 1988 gassing of five thousand Kurds at Halabja, U.S. aid *continued;* the gas attack became a useful talking point only years later, after Saddam invaded Kuwait. Rumsfeld was an integral part of creating these policies. Concern for Iraqi civilians? Sadly, nonsense.

Why the rush to war? Everybody involved probably had their own reasons: ideology, revenge, religious furor, bad advice, profiteering, groupthink, and sheer incompetence suggest themselves. Whatever, it's costing U.S. taxpayers $2 billion *per week,* a sum ten times larger than maintaining the defanged-Saddam status quo.

The human cost, meanwhile, is beyond calculation. While Americans typically guess the Iraqi death toll at under 10,000, as of early 2007, the minimum figure exceeds 50,000. The high end, using the same methodology taught by the U.S. government, used uncontroversially in Kosovo and Afghanistan, and supported by the chief scientific advisor to the British Ministry of Defence, estimates over 600,000.

Now that you feel like throwing up, let's look at the players:

SUNNIS

Sunni Arabs are only about 15 percent of Iraq's population, living mostly between the Tigris and the Euphrates, north of Baghdad. Saddam Hussein was a nonreligious Sunni, although he made public displays of Islam after the 1991 U.S. invasion. Outnumbered by the Shi'a majority, Saddam populated his government and military with fellow Sunnis.

There are three main reasons Sunnis have fought the U.S.: (a) rebellion against occupation, with occasional loyalty to the former regime; (b) Sunni nationalism, coupled with a fear of the Shi'a-dominated government resulting from any democracy; and (c) for extremists, Islamist jihad. However, while Al-Qaeda usually draws from puritan Sunni extremists, most Iraqi Sunnis remain unsympathetic. Many are even actively hostile (see "Al-Qaeda," p. 25).

SHI'A

Shi'a were directly oppressed before Saddam even came into power; Shi'a areas were battlegrounds during both the horrible 1980–88

WHAT'S THE DIFFERENCE BETWEEN SHI'A AND SUNNI?

From a distance, about as much as between Catholic and Protestant. Which means: enough to live in peace or get lots of people killed.

Both branches worship the same god, praise the same prophets, make the same pilgrimage to Mecca, and use the same Koran. Shi'a are a bit more like Catholics, interposing a hierarchy of imams and ayatollahs between the worshipper and the infinite. Sunnis are more like Protestants, with greater emphasis on the book and the path.

Unlike Christianity, the split here happened from the get-go, shortly after Muhammad died, in an argument over his rightful successor. The conflict over who can rightly claim the truest pipeline to Allah has lasted 1,327 years. So far. Believers often see only the differences, with messy results.

Sunnis outnumber Shi'a worldwide by at least six to one, although Shi'a are in the majority in Iran, Iraq, and a few other places. It's not uncommon for the local majority to oppress the minority, either way.

Fortunately, also like Protestants and Catholics, communities of Sunni and Shi'a can get along just fine. When they're not murdering each other.

war with Iran and the 1991 U.S.-led response to the occupation of Kuwait; and all of Iraq was subject to international sanctions for a decade thereafter. All told, things for your average Iraqi Shi'a have sucked longer than many can even remember.

However, Shi'a Arabs comprise about 65 percent of Iraq, mostly in the south along the Iranian border. In any democracy (or total chaos for that matter), Shi'a would probably dominate. Since Iran is mostly Shi'a as well, one main effect of the 2003 invasion was to hand increased power to Iran on a silver platter. (Not surprisingly, several of the trusted anti-Saddam opposition leaders who promised White House ideologues a cakewalk were tight with Tehran all along.) After the invasion, Iran quickly began to arm Shi'a militias, most notably the Mahdi Army, headquartered in a Baghdad slum called Sadr City and headed by Moqtada al-Sadr.

The Mahdi Army has staged several anti-U.S. uprisings, but of late is also becoming a more Hezbollah-like presence (see "Israel and Friends," p. 34), serving as a Shi'a political and social welfare organization. In addition to the shooting and the killing.

KURDS

Iraq's Kurdish minority—about 20 percent of the population—are ethnically, culturally, and religiously distinct from other Iraqis, not to mention Arabs, Turks, and Iranians. Kurds never got a Kurdistan under British colonial rule; Britain didn't want to encourage other minorities in the oil-rich south. As a result, Kurds have long been a large minority in three different countries (see "Turkey," p. 42, and "Iran," p. 29) who see Kurds as political pawns if not enemies of the state.

In 1987–89, Saddam's army flattened more than a thousand Kurdish villages; the word *genocide* has been suggested for less. But after the first Gulf War in 1991, the UN imposed a "safe haven" for Kurds, enforced by a no-fly zone. Soon, Iraq's north became a quasi-autonomous

Iraqi Kurdistan, outside Saddam's control. (The exact boundaries currently under Kurdistan Regional Government control seem to depend on whom you ask; consider the map a best guess.) Since Kirkuk has boatloads of oil, the Kurds could likely sustain real independence. Unfortunately for them, it's not in any other nation's self-interest.

AL-QAEDA

In mid–2002, Al-Qaeda was largely defeated in Pakistan's mountains. Inside Iraq, a handful of sympathizers, Ansar al-Islam, operated in Kurdistan, outside of Saddam's control. (This was one of the vaunted "links" between Saddam and Osama; a U.S. Senate investigation later concluded that Saddam viewed Ansar al-Islam not as an ally, but a threat.) Ansar was only tangential to the Big Bad, and after the 2003 invasion of Iraq, Ansar was driven over the Iranian border by U.S. and Kurdish forces. End of story. Except . . .

With U.S. troops occupying an unstable country, Al-Qaeda sympathizers now had something handy to shoot at, plus a marvelous local recruiting tool. *After* the invasion—not before—a Jordanian veteran of the Afghan mujahedin, Abu Musab al-Zarqawi, pulled together fighters originally recruited to overthrow the Jordanian government, plus some muj buddies and Ansar leftovers. Thus, "Al-Qaeda in Iraq."

Al-Qaeda in Iraq has since become a regional force in Al Anbar, which would be worse if more of it were actually populated. As in other Sunni regions, Al-Qaeda enhances its stature by pushing the Sunni/Shi'a civil war, attracting Sunnis by provoking animosity and violence with Shi'a, especially in Baghdad.

However, Al-Qaeda has only a tenuous alliance at best with some Sunni insurgents, who tend to be more nationalist and less Islamist. Some Sunnis are understandably suspicious of Al-Qaeda foreigners showing up, blowing up, and cutting in line for the seventy-two virgins. Lots of Iraqi Sunnis can't stand them. So while new Al-Qaeda groups do pop up, "Al-Qaeda in such-and-such," only a small percentage of Iraq's suicide bombers are native. Almost half come from Saudi Arabia, Al-Qaeda's most fertile recruiting ground.

Speaking of Saudi Arabia: It's home to Mecca and Medina, two of Islam's holiest cities, and recent site of several U.S. military bases. (This was a major pisser for Al-Qaeda.) Saudi Arabia is also the birthplace of Osama, fifteen of the 9-11 hijackers, and almost half of the suicide bombers in Iraq; Saudi money also finances the Taliban and Islamist madrasahs. Not coincidentally, the Saudi dictatorship practices judicial beheadings, whippings, stonings, mutilations, and even crucifixions.* Yet the Saudi monarchy is a close ally not just of the White House, but of the Bushes, personally. Bandar bin Sultan, son of the Saudi crown prince, has been a trusted Bush family advisor—nicknamed "Bandar Bush," in fact—for twenty years; Bandar's input was key to soliciting Saudi Arabia's reluctant support for the invasion. The BBC has reported that Bandar has also personally received perhaps a billion dollars in bribes from military interests. Small world.

And in early 2007, according to the Bush administration's own Director of National Intelligence, Saudi money has begun funding Sunni extremist militias in Iraq. Yes, those would be the same militias recently so fond of attacking U.S. troops.

The reason for this madness? Alongside everything else, Iraq may be evolving into a proxy war between Saudi Arabia and Iran. Put simply: the Saudis arm the Sunnis, Iran cranks up the Shi'a, and the winner gets the oil in the middle, or at least hegemony over a bigger share.

And *that's* where U.S. troops sit, with no clear objective, no exit

---

*Full disclosure: I used to work with members of the Saudi army, several of whom I liked very much. I may be going soft on the Saudis here.

strategy, and a shifting array of targets. Almost three-quarters of U.S. army brigades have already done multiple tours in Iraq, Afghanistan, or both. With no end in sight.

As to a war on terrorism: not even counting Iraq and Afghanistan, where such incidents have skyrocketed, Islamist political violence against Western targets is *up* 25 percent worldwide since 2003. Thanks to the ill-conceived invasion, Iraq is now a proving ground for the development and export of well-armed extremism much like Afghanistan two decades ago. The shaky Saudi dictatorship recently arrested over 170 men plotting a massive series of attacks. Even Western Europe now faces a rising influx of their own Muslim citizens, radicalized and returning from Iraq.

Had the U.S. simply pursued Al-Qaeda where it was—finishing the war in Afghanistan when America had the world's sympathies— Saddam would still be contained, Al-Qaeda would be crushed, international Islamism would not have Iraq as a global recruiting tool, and every regional government would probably be much more stable.

Instead, Bin Laden stated that one of the goals of 9-11 was to provoke an overreaction which would improve Al-Qaeda's standing and ability to recruit. *Check.* And after Zarqawi was killed, some of his documents revealed that one of his major goals was to entice the U.S. into war with Iran—again, strengthening the extremists' hand. In early 2007, the White House is ramping up hostilities with Iran. *Check.*

Yet despite the obvious complexity of the situation, U.S. debate often speaks of "Iraqis" as one people, while reducing America's options to "stay the course" or "withdraw." In biology, this simple two-pronged response mechanism is called "fight-or-flight." Sadly, much current U.S. political debate is only marginally more complex than what goes on in the preconscious mind of a baboon, confronted by another baboon.

It's not obvious what the U.S. should do next. It's also hard to reassemble a house of cards that someone has burned down, although you could have figured the blowtorch was a bad idea. Clearly, the invasion has unleashed a civil war that the U.S. cannot unilaterally end; meanwhile, the presence of U.S. troops is itself a radicalizing force, creating additional enemies where Al-Qaeda is unlikely to flourish otherwise. Given that the vast majority of Iraqis want the U.S. to leave—and it *is* their country—this may be a rational choice. Assuming we want to be rational.

Whether or not Iraq devolves into Kurdish, Sunni, and Shi'a entities, the main question is how to minimize bloodshed and doom while deciding on the map. Since no single government (including the U.S.) can possibly impose a solution, a regional approach—incorporating Saudi Arabia, Iran, Syria, Turkey, and local leaders, all committed to resolving muliple issues at once—might be the only real hope for peace.

Given the recent behavior of every single government in that list, we should probably expect further hell.

IRAN

- Official hostility toward Israel
- Iranian-armed Shi'a v. Sunnis in Iraq (proxy)
- Severe repression of Bahá'í faith and other dissidents
- Kurdish and miscellaneous separatist groups v. Tehran
- Tehran v. Washington (looming, as of early 2007)

Since *hate* is in this book's title, let's begin with the 2006 Festival of Holocaust Denial, wherein president Mahmoud Ahmadinejad invited the world's leading crackpots for a shindig of wrongitude. The claimed agenda was a questioning of Zionism, not Judaism per se, although the Holocaust-questioning thing sure bent that line. Jetting the former head of the Ku Klux Klan halfway around the world for tea is legitimately creepy.

Still, about 25,000 Jews do live in Iran, and Judaism is officially recognized, so synagogues practice without fear. However, Jews are second-class citizens, Zionist views are verboten, and Iranian Jews are forbidden from important jobs in the government, judiciary, and elsewhere. (So are other religious minorities.) The anti-Israel thing is intense enough that in 2003, when the Iranian city of Bam was crushed by an earthquake, killing thousands, Tehran refused Israel's help. So when Ahmadinejad goes all Lex Luthor about Israel vanishing from the pages of time, your ears perk up, rightly so.

But you can't judge any entire nation by its leader. In 2005, Ahmadinejad got less than 20 percent of the first ballot; while he won the runoff, he's sure not terribly popular. The economy sucks, unemployment is up, and Iranian parliament members have decried Ahmadinejad's militant posturing as a cheap attempt to distract Iran from domestic issues. Meanwhile, *real* power rests with the Supreme Leader and his Guardian Council; every law and elected official needs their approval.

Ayatollah Ali Khamenei, current Supreme-Leader-for-life, shouldn't be confused with Ayatollah Ruhollah Khomeini, but you wouldn't be far off the mark. One of Khamenei's favorite advisors is a Koran literalist who has no problem with violence in defense of Islam. Still, Khamenei harshly condemned the 9-11 attacks, and thousands of Iranians held candlelight vigils.

Obviously, you can't equate Ahmadinejad with Iran's government, much less its millions of people, despite the impression given by recent U.S. news broadcasts. And minority unrest is common, despite violent repression.

The Bahá'í faith, a pacifist spinoff of Islam as threatening as a Seals & Crofts concert, is intensely oppressed.* After the 1979 revolution, Iran's 300,000 Bahá'ís had property confiscated, shrines demolished, and leaders executed. They're still reportedly monitored like spies.

Shi'a Azeris (aka Azerbaijanis) are well accepted, but Sunnis in Baluchistan complain their language and culture have been suppressed for generations; a rebel army is now active across the Pakistan border. To the southwest, dozens of Arabs were killed in 2005 demonstrations in Khuzestan, smack-dab astride Iran's coastal oil reserves. To the north, Kurds desire an independent Kurdistan—already a reality in Iraq, where Iranian Kurds have built an insurgency that reportedly receives U.S. funding.

Speaking of which: Iran's elected government was overthrown in

---

*I used to date a Bahá'í girl; rest assured, the only violence Bahá'ís espouse is death by tranquillity.

1953 by the CIA, and under the Shah's secret police, "poker night" involved the fireplace implement, not playing cards. (The current regime is even worse on human rights; the qualitative difference is that the Shah's cops would beat women for *not* dressing like Westerners.) This is often forgotten in the United States. Not in Iran.

With U.S. troops throughout the region, from Iran's POV, the U.S. has Iran almost surrounded. Not surprising, then, that Iran would ignore U.S. interests and push for a Shi'a government in Iraq by any means, including covert arming of Shi'a factions. Iran needs a stable, pro-Shi'a Iraq rather desperately; a failed Iraq promises Kurdish unrest, an influx of Shi'a refugees, and a civil war that could cross the border. In a saner world, the U.S. and Iran would see Iraq's stability as a common interest.

Iran's claim that its nuclear program is peaceful doesn't seem likely. However, Iran's energy infrastructure *is* crap enough that they import almost half of their gas, they do save most of their crude for export, and the Ayatollah has issued a fatwa against nuclear weapons. Either way, Iran still spins the uranium, defying the UN by grasping for 21st-century power in a state built around 7th-century ideology.

At this writing, the Pentagon has sent extra ships to the Gulf, White House spokesmen are using increasingly confrontational rhetoric, and the U.S. president has refused to rule out a "limited" strike on Iran's atomic facilities. (Disturbingly, CIA and Pentagon wargames reportedly indicate that escalation would be almost inevitable. The long-term consequences could make Iraq look like a fender bender.) Meanwhile, Iran has tested a new missile system with the capacity to strike U.S. ships in the Gulf; this wasn't a big deal in the U.S. media, however, because it happened on the same day that Anna Nicole Smith died. (I swear.)

U.S. officials have also accused Iran of covert attacks against U.S. troops inside Iraq; while there's no question that Iran is supporting the major Shi'a militias, evidence of direct Iranian intervention has so far been thoroughly half-assed. Meanwhile, anti-Iranian separatists have staged attacks from Iraqi territory, and minority unrest across Iran has spiked; Tehran has accused the U.S. of trying to destabilize Iran, a charge that became more plausible after mainstream news reports of CIA operations to, um, destabilize Iran. Next thing you know, Iran is cracking down on student and union leaders (not to mention women wearing skirts), trumping up charges against several Iranian-Americans, and off we go.

In early 2007, however, Iran played catch-and-release with fifteen UK Marines, and nobody shot anybody. Strange. Maybe the mutual accusations are partly just posturing for domestic consumption in both Iran and the West. Maybe much-needed talks are still possible. Let's hope.

In any case, with an economy in shreds and social repression so severe that Ahmadinejad himself got in hot water just for politely kissing an old woman's hand, Iran's brightest young minds are leaving in droves, with perhaps 150,000 of the country's best-educated youth fleeing each year.

Long-term, the regime's future may be going with them.

ISRAEL AND FRIENDS

- Israel v. various Arab neighbors, six decades, off and on
- Israel v. the PLO in Israel, the West Bank, Gaza, Jordan, and Lebanon, three decades
- Israel v. Hezbollah in Israel and Lebanon, two decades
- Israel v. Hamas in the West Bank and Israel, two decades

(**N**ote: I feel especially compelled to disavow any expertise here, since well-funded think tanks on each side are brilliant at assembling selected facts to buttress their case, often on cable TV. Everything below will likely be contradicted by someone with deeper knowledge and better hair. So please assume that every word in this entry is factually wrong, including the word *word*.)

When speaking with anyone who is stridently pro- or anti-Israel, I'm always struck by how each side seems to see entirely different maps of the world, legitimately justifying a sense of perpetual self-defense:

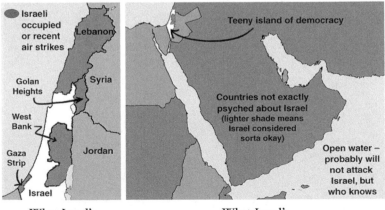

What Israel's opponents see

What Israel's supporters see

After WWII, as the region was emerging from colonial rule, the UN decided on side-by-side Jewish and Arab Palestinian states. The soon-to-be Israelis loved it, but the Arab nations didn't—and so in 1948, Egypt, Iraq, Syria, Lebanon, and friends sent in troops, hoping to strangle the infant nation in its crib. To their surprise, Israel fought back, eventually taking almost 50 percent more territory than originally planned. Whoops. Almost sixty years later, many Arab nations and factions still refuse to recognize Israel's legitimacy. Israel has barely known a moment of real peace and security in its entire history. So when Israel's supporters say that they're surrounded, well, yes.

The war drove roughly two-thirds of the Palestinian Arab population—about 700,000 people—out of Israeli-held territory. The truce was supposed to allow refugees the right of return, but Israel refused, since Israelis would have been outnumbered (and probably still would be, if a full right of return were ever implemented). Israel's government also demolished what was left of many Palestinian villages and passed laws allowing the confiscation of property left behind. So when Palestinian civilians say that they were shoved off their land and that their property was seized, they have a point, too.

Meanwhile, Arab countries to which Palestinians fled rarely assimilated them, partly because doing so would help finalize Israel's victory. Even now, vast masses of Palestinians still have only refugee status in Jordan, Syria, and Lebanon. (Then again, Jordan has also granted citizenship to so many Palestinians that they may now outnumber native Jordanians.) So when Israel's supporters respond that the Arab countries shouldn't have started the 1948 war, and that afterward, they might have accepted their Palestinian brothers at some point in the last half-century, you can see their point, too.

In 1967, Israel and its neighbors engaged in a spasm called the Six Day War, resulting in Israel's seizure of the West Bank from Jordan, the Sinai peninsula and Gaza Strip from Egypt, and the Golan Heights from

Syria. Israel had a legitimate security interest in holding these territories; the Gaza Strip, for example, had been used by Egypt to stage literally thousands of small attacks on Israel, although Egypt never allowed the Palestinians anything like an actual home. (Incidentally, your ordinary Palestinian, the Yousef Sixpack who just wants a decent life, really does seem to have been totally screwed from pretty much all sides.)

In 1973, Egypt and Syria tried a sneak attack across the Sinai and Golan Heights; despite early success, before long, the Israelis had not only repelled the attacks but pushed outward to within twenty-five miles of Damascus and sixty-five miles of Cairo, even trapping one of Egypt's armies on the wrong side of the Suez. Conventional war against Israel stopped looking like such a hot idea.

In 1979, Egyptian president Anwar Sadat won from Israel through diplomacy what could not be gained via force: the Sinai, thanks to a series of accords signed at Camp David and brokered by Jimmy Carter. This was the first formal peace treaty between any Arab state and Israel; the peace has lasted for nearly thirty years. More, the treaty demonstrated a useful "land for peace" model for negotiations.

Unfortunately, peace didn't exactly catch on elsewhere. To the east, the Palestinian Liberation Organization (PLO; actually an umbrella of numerous smaller factions) rose to prominence after the defeat of formal Arab armies in the Six Day War. When Yassir Arafat's secular nationalist faction, Fatah,* gained control of the PLO in 1969, Arafat became the face of Palestinians to the world.

Originally based in Jordan, Arafat's PLO not only attacked Israel but also set itself up as a de facto government in Palestinian areas of Jordan. Israel's retaliations inevitably got Jordanians killed, eventually

---

*Not to be confused with Fatah al-Islam, a recent small knot of Iraq-hardened Islamist militants based in a Palestinian refugee camp in Lebanon.

leading to conflict between the PLO and Jordan, too. The end result: in 1970, the PLO moved to Syria and Lebanon, putting down roots in the latter, where numerous Palestinians had also fled after 1948. Lebanon sank into its own civil war in 1975, but Arafat's home office remained in West Beirut, and his PLO made southern Lebanon a new base for attacks against Israel.

In 1978, a Fatah bus hijacking resulted in the deaths of 37 Israelis. Israel responded by invading southern Lebanon, driving perhaps 100,000 Lebanese from their homes. Israel eventually withdrew, but PLO attacks continued, since a UN cease-fire applied only to the Lebanese border, and the PLO could still attack from the east. Israeli defense minister Ariel Sharon sought to knock out the PLO for good, so in 1982, he ordered a full-scale invasion of Lebanon and bombing raids on West Beirut. Amid much international hollering, Israel and the PLO both agreed to withdraw (the PLO eventually relocated to Tunisia), with U.S. and other allied troops keeping the peace. However, Sharon believed that thousands of PLO fighters were still hiding in refugee camps outside Beirut, so he sent in a proxy force of Lebanese militia to root them out; after three days of awfulness, perhaps 2,000 Palestinians were dead. Few if any were PLO fighters.

By now, Israel (and by extension, the United States, upon whose aid Israel relied) was considered an enemy not just by Palestinians, but by multiple Lebanese factions. Since many Shi'a youths had been inspired by the 1979 Iranian revolution, Iran sent soldiers to train Shi'a militias in Beirut. The eventual result: Hezbollah ("Party of God"). Another result: the U.S. Embassy in Beirut in flames. Also, a U.S. Marine barracks. Plus, continued war for Israel, as Hezbollah began suicide attacks against Israeli military and civilian targets.

Despite originally planning to turn Lebanon into an Islamist state, over the years, Hezbollah has refocused more on fighting Israel while consolidating its support at home. So from Hezbollah, the West gets assassinations, bombings, and mass violence, but Lebanese Shi'a get schools, food, hospitals, security, and financial services. (If this seems schizophrenic, well, yeah. But from Hezbollah's point of view, this is not so different from what Western governments offer their own enemies and citizens.)

By the late 1980s a similar Sunni movement, Hamas, arose among Palestinians in the Gaza Strip, offering suicide attacks to outsiders and day care to insiders. More hell for Israel. Moreover, Hamas is as Islamist as Fatah is secular, seeing the struggle to recapture Israel as their god's will. (Contrast with the Israeli belief that *their* god gave the land to *them*.)

Arafat, now declawed, began talking up a two-state solution, and in 1993, the PLO and Israel signed the Oslo Accords, recognizing each other's legitimacy. Palestinians also gained limited autonomy in the Gaza Strip, with a new Palestinian Authority (which was still run by Arafat) as a five-year transitional organization to oversee Palestinian affairs while further details of the West Bank were hammered out.

However, subsequent negotiations have failed to get anywhere. Talks at Camp David in 2000 broke down over the right of return (or compensation, in its place), control over shrines in East Jerusalem, and Israel's settlements in the occupied territories.

The settlements have essentially been a slow colonization of the West Bank with Israeli communities; until recently, settlers received large tax breaks to move in. Most observers consider these settlements a violation of international law. Israel disagrees, treating some settlement areas for security purposes as essentially part of Israel proper—resulting in big walls, huge security hassles, and a bizarrely shaped border at the West Bank frontier. More on that shortly.

Arafat was widely blamed in the West for the breakdown of talks. But whomever one blames, the settlements seem to have been the main sticking point; indeed, Israel's land-for-peace offer to the Palestinians differed from the one that succeeded twenty-one years earlier; while Israel had offered Egypt the full Sinai, Israel only offered the Palestinians less than three-quarters of the West Bank to start, with the settlements remaining mostly intact. At another summit in Taba in 2001, both sides arrived with multiple maps of the West Bank, trying to sort out who needed what. Sadly, they never did.

In any case, not every Palestinian faction bought into Oslo—Hamas being the prime example—so violence against Israel never stopped. After Ariel Sharon became Israeli prime minister two months after George W. Bush took office in the United States, neither was willing to deal with Arafat, despite Oslo. This didn't help create peace. The Palestinian Authority, founded thirteen years earlier as a five-year project for peace, returned to hostility in 2006, after Fatah lost control to Islamist Hamas. The aftermath included dreadful Palestinian infighting, hundreds if not thousands of deaths, and a disavowal of the Palestinian Authority throughout much of the West.

To the north, Israel and Hezbollah fought another war in 2006, beginning when a Hezbollah incursion killed three Israeli soldiers. The Israeli response included an air and naval blockade, major air strikes, a ground invasion, and the destruction of large amounts of civilian infrastructure. The war led to well over a thousand deaths—almost 90 percent of them Lebanese, most of them civilians—and the displacement of hundreds of thousands of civilians on both sides. For its part, Hezbollah's rockets hit hospitals, rail yards, and the occasional military target. Israel fought bigger, but nobody here fought nice.

The Israelis apparently hoped to destroy Hezbollah's missile threat or cut into its support in Lebanon. Within six months, however, Hezbollah had rearmed, becoming even more popular in Lebanon than it had been before the war.

Meanwhile, an Israeli government report later found that the prime minister rushed into an ill-planned war, resulting in needless tragedy. Massive protests followed, although resignations did not. Israeli democracy appears to be both thriving and deeply dysfunctional. This should feel familiar to U.S. readers.

So what's next? The Syrian border, at least, has been stable for decades, but Syria's ties to Iran and support for Hamas and Hezbollah violence would have to cease for Israel to consider a deal on the Golan Heights. Hezbollah's leadership has actually grunted about begrudging coexistence with Israel, pending the release of prisoners, mutual security, and so on. However, because it's Hezbollah, the West generally dismisses this out of hand. Whether that's good or bad is your call.

As to the Palestinians, in early 2007, Hamas and Fatah agreed to forgo their animosity and present a united front. At the time, the agreement was virtually ignored in Western broadcast media because it happened the same day Anna Nicole Smith died. (I swear.) Of the two, Hamas remains the more bellicose. One Hamas-produced children's TV show even used a Mickey Mouse–like character named Butterfly to teach Palestinian kids to kill and die for the cause.

Is peace even possible? Jimmy Carter, a Nobel Peace Prize laureate who moderated the most important peace deal in Israel's history, noted in 2006 that UN resolutions, the Camp David Accords, and Oslo all called for Israel to withdraw fully from the occupied territories. Carter also said that for Israel to do so, they'll need to feel secure, so the Palestinians (and all other players) will have to recognize Israel's right to exist, something virtually every Arab nation has expressed some willingness to do—*if* Israel withdraws to pre-1967 borders.

Unfortunately, Carter's suggestions weren't discussed in the West nearly as much as his book's title, which contained the word *apartheid* in a provocative reference to the occupied territories. For this, he was called an anti-Semite. Obviously, the man who brokered Israel's lasting peace with Egypt did so because he *hated Jews*. Oy.

(Incidentally, in February 2007, John Dugard, a judge from the

International Court of Justice working as the UN's Special Rapporteur on the Occupied Territories, described the West Bank as "worse than . . . in South Africa." Dugard is a seventy-one-year-old South African professor of international law who lived through the entire apartheid era, personally observing its practice in Johannesburg, firsthand, on a daily basis. He is also the author of several books and legal briefs on South African apartheid. But what does he know?)

Fairly or not, the word *apartheid* has arisen largely because of a massive 420-mile-long barrier Israel has been building roughly along the border between Israel and the West Bank, with some sections built directly on (and therefore taking) extra chunks of West Bank land. Israel says this improves their security, and this is obviously true; suicide bombings have dropped precipitously since the wall's construction began. But Palestinians and many international observers say that the wall has also split innocent families, damaged farmlands, further isolated East Jerusalem from the rest of the West Bank, and caused serious economic hardship for countless Palestinians, and this is obviously true, too. So whether the wall will lead to long-term peace—possibly as Israel's attempt at a unilateral solution—or to further hatred is hotly debated, with opinions depending quite literally on whose side you're on.

Update: As this goes to print, the accord between Hamas and Fatah has disintegrated. Hamas has seized Gaza, Fatah rules the West Bank, and the two-state solution again appears dead. Meanwhile, Hamas TV producers have killed off Butterfly, telling children he died a martyr at the hands of Israel. Hope may require even greater imagination.

TURKEY

*I will struggle so the Kurdish and Turkish peoples
may live together in a democratic framework.*
—LAYLA ZANA, MEMBER OF PARLIAMENT,
IN KURDISH; SHE SPENT NEARLY TEN YEARS
IN PRISON FOR THIS STATEMENT

- Ankara v. Kurdish separatists
- Turkish radicals v. Armenians, Kurds, and Turks who speak too
  freely
- Low-level angst with Greece over Cyprus
- Increasing dislike of the United States, the United Kingdom, and
  Israel over Iraq

T he Ottoman Empire, Turkey's predecessor, once ruled things from the edge of Austria all the way to modern Algeria. Despite this, under Ottoman law, a "Turk" was a Muslim of any ethnicity. The empire splintered partly due to ethnic nationalism, which is part of why Turkish law still bans ethnic political parties. The country's minorities, then, have a diminished ability to respond to ethnic *Turkish* activism. And this can be virulent.

During WWI, the Ottomans got whopped by Russia, but they blamed the Armenians. So starting in 1915, roughly a million Armenians (estimates vary), most from the eastern half of present-day Turkey, died in a forced march that pushed them into the countryside—or even the Syrian desert—to die of thirst, hunger, and disease. Many were massacred before they even got that far. (The Turkish version claims a much lower death count, attributing the deaths to wartime conditions. The word *genocide* may be debated, but Adolf Hitler himself took notice of this successful forced removal of an internal "enemy" with speed, thoroughness, and impunity. Tells you something.)

To this day, Turkish writers examine this only at great risk. Nobel Prize–winning novelist Orhan Pamuk and journalist Hrant Dink were both recently prosecuted for "insulting" the nation by merely discussing the issue. Both were deluged with threats, and Dink was killed by an assassin tied to radical Turkish nationalists.

Cyprus is another good subject not to bring up around nationalists, both here and in Greece. How's this for a grudge? The Greek national costume has four hundred pleats—one for every year of Turkish occupation—and Greek tourist maps of the Aegean islands often replace Turkey with open sea.

When the UK granted independence to most of Cyprus, its Greek majority tried to unify the island with Greece. Turkey not only intervened to protect the Turkish minority, it grabbed extra land, imported tens of thousands of new settlers, and proclaimed the entirely new and separate nation of Northern Cyprus, recognized by no other government on earth. More Turks now live on Cyprus than in the first place, many on land Greek Cypriots still claim. There is little chance of war in Cyprus, but also little chance of peace.

Nationalists and more moderate Turks have also been hostile for decades toward Kurdish separatism, especially the Kurdistan Workers Party (PKK in Turkish), founded in 1978 by Abdullah Öcalan, which spent more than twenty years engaging in assassinations, suicide bombings, and assorted carnage. Ankara responded by shoving over at least a million Kurds (again, estimates vary) out of rural villages in the east, hoping to cut off PKK support. Entire towns were demolished. Elsewhere, pro-government militias ("Village Guards") were recruited and armed; human rights groups say the Guards often "disappeared" suspected PKK sympathizers. About 37,000 people, mostly Kurds, died.

The Turks captured Öcalan in 1999. Faced with the death penalty himself, Öcalan suddenly began calling for peaceful solutions. However, a radical splinter faction, the Kurdistan Freedom Falcons (TAK), has begun bombing popular areas around Istanbul and the Aegean coast, hoping to diminish tourism and hit Ankara in the wallet.

Words seem oddly terrifying here. Zoologists are asked not to use Latin species names that refer to Armenia or Kurdistan. The entire Kurdish language was once banned; a Member of Parliament was jailed for nearly a decade just for speaking in Kurdish. And when the mayor of Batman (a fine place-name, that) tried to rename local roads to Human Rights Boulevard and Gandhi Street, Ankara forbade it, lest this encourage Kurdish unrest. In fact, this elected government wouldn't allow Democracy Avenue.

Hundreds of thousands of Kurds reportedly remain dislocated, and there are numerous reports of their abuse by Village Guards, but Ankara has at least given an inch: two TV channels can now broadcast

Hitler shares an
Istanbul bookseller's
table space with
Steinbeck.

in Kurdish, and the language may be taught in schools, albeit on a strictly limited basis.

However, *Mein Kampf* not only is *not* banned, it's popular. Sales sky-rocketed after the U.S. invasion of Iraq. A bookseller I spoke with said this was a mixture of anger at Israel, the U.S., and the UK; curiosity at the forbidden; and the cheap price of bootleg Turkish editions.

Anger at the United States has many causes, most rooted in the Iraq invasion. Muslim Turks identify with Iraqi casualties. The PKK has safe haven in Iraqi Kurdistan, which the U.S. now influences, and Kurdistan-based separatist violence continues, so the U.S. gets blamed. (A Turkish incursion into Iraqi Kurdistan is even possible.) The U.S. has rotated troops via Incirlik Air Base, despite Turkish opposition. Worst of all, in 2003, U.S. troops grabbed eleven Turkish soldiers in

Kurdistan and gang-marched them around with their heads in sacks like Gitmo prisoners. In Turkey, it's still a source of fury. A 2004 novel called *Metal Storm,* in which Turkey and Germany nuke the U.S., outsold even *Mein Kampf.*

In 2006, the most expensive film in Turkish history, *Valley of the Wolves: Iraq,* portrayed not just the head-bagging and other real stuff like Abu Ghraib, Gitmo, and the massacre of a civilian wedding after celebratory gunfire; it also included the deranged sight of Gary Busey playing a Jewish doctor harvesting Iraqi organs for sale on the black markets of New York and Tel Aviv. This blood libel opened bigger than any film in Turkish history, breaking the previous box office record by 40 percent, and winning approval from Turkey's prime minister.

Bizarre, I know. (Gary Busey, playing a *doctor?*) So the Turkish view of the United States may be just a teeny bit wack.

Then again, more than a million Turks—mostly Muslims—recently rallied in the streets of Istanbul, supporting purely secular democracy over Islamism. But most Americans my age think of Turkey as looking entirely like the film *Midnight Express.*

Fair's fair.

BONUS STRESS:
SORTING OUT THE STANS

Russia

Note: in no way should this shape remind you of a mushroom cloud

STANISTAN

Kazakh-

Kyrgyz-

Uzbeki-

Turkmeni-

Tajiki-

Caspian Sea

China

Azerbaijan

Iran

Afghani-

Paki-

Nepal

Saudi Arabia

India

he suffix -*stan* just means "land of the" in Persian-derived languages; it's synonymous with -*land* in *Iceland* (land of ice), *Poland* (land of Poles), and *Ireland* (land of ire; see "United Kingdom," p. 193). Since Persian is an Indo-European tongue, this -*stan* business probably shares the same root as our own word *stand*, as in defending one's home. Similar noises mean the same thing in German, Latin, Greek, Russian, and even Sanskrit. Our planet is teeny.

47

Of the seven current full-blown Stan nations, the two southern-most were messed with most by the UK, while the five closest to Russia were Soviet republics.

All seven Stans feature Sunni Islam as the largest religion. In the former Soviet Stans, the Russian Orthodox Church is the biggest minority religion, with Tajikistan as the exception. In Tajikistan, Afghanistan, and Pakistan, Shi'a Islam is second.

Russian is still widely spoken in all five former Soviet states, but the primary local languages are indeed Kazakh, Turkmen, Uzbek, Tajik, and Kyrgyz. Four of those are Turkic languages, and fairly closely related. (It used to be said that knowing Turkish could get you to China on the Silk Road; the map shows why.)

The exception again is Tajik, a dialect of Persian. Various Persian empires pushed thisaway about the time Michelangelo was painting the Sistine Chapel thataway. Until the British showed up, Persian languages reached the edge of China and as far south as India; Persian dialects are still spoken in a continuous belt from Iran to Tajikistan.

The five former Soviet Republics still struggle economically, but the two bordering on the oil-rich Caspian have about four times the per capita GDP of the others, despite serious corruption. Here's each one, offensively and irresponsibly oversimplified:

In *Turkmenistan,* the dictator built a bizarre cult of personality, banning opera and beards, renaming the month of April for his mom ("Gurbansoltanedzhe," which has a real ring), and encouraging children to chew on bones to build their teeth. After this dictator dropped dead, he was replaced in a rigged election by his former dentist, whose name in English contains more than half of our alphabet, including every vowel. (Really.)

Kazakhstan is richer still, attracting lots of foreign investment. It's more diverse than the other former Soviet Stans, and folks generally get along, but a yawning gulf is starting to open between rich and poor. Its dictator is dutiful about staging rigged elections, but his family owns most of the media, and speaking ill of him is a criminal offense. Not surprisingly, the foreign ministry denounced the film *Borat* as "utterly unacceptable," although one of the president's daughters has said, "We should not be afraid of humor." At last report, she is still alive.

By contrast, what *Uzbekistan* lacks in wealth it makes up for in extra dictatorship. Dissidents have been tortured and sometimes massacred. Repression is rationalized because the most visible opponents are Islamist extremists, some of whom have joined up actively with Al-Qaeda in Waziristan (see "Afghanistan/Pakistan," p. 11). Perhaps not surprisingly, Uzbekistan's government is tight with the White House. However, they've tortured thousands of people, and the UK ambassador says some have been boiled alive.

Kyrgyzstan is also poor, but it's the most free and least religious of the Stans. After the Soviet breakup, this Stan had a much-less-horrible government than the others, and even that was overthrown by a not-very-violent "Tulip Revolution" that led to somewhat-less-rigged elections. So, progress.

Tajikistan is the youngest Stan, with half the population under fifteen. Not coincidentally (see "Conclusion," p. 211), this is the only former Soviet Stan to have had a major civil war, staged between pro-Russian militias and an unusual alliance of Islamists and democratic liberals. Tens of thousands died before the UN chilled things in 1997. Its southern border is a frequent site of smuggling from Afghanistan.

Speaking of *Afghanistan,* Britain spent a good deal of the 19th century trying to keep the Russians from gaining influence there, a struggle historians call "The Great Game." The UK worried that Russia might come after its holdings in British India (which included modern Pakistan), so they tried to create a buffer by imposing a hand-picked ruler in Kabul. This got lots of British soldiers killed. It also got more of them killed when they tried it again forty years later. However, the Afghan ruler was shaky enough that he let the UK run his foreign affairs, a deal that lasted for about forty more years—during which the UK drew the boundary with Pakistan specifically to split up the Afghan people, sticking two-thirds of the Pashtuns south of the line. Finally, starting in 1919, the Afghans killed even more British soldiers, and the British bailed back into India.

The word *Pakistan* was invented in the 1930s as an acronym for its Muslim peoples: *P*unjabis, *A*fghans, *K*ashmirs, *S*indhs, and Baluchis*tan* squeezed in on the end. Not perfect, but college kids made it up, and it also means "land of the pure" in three languages. Students were inventing such names because Muslims in British India realized that independence might leave them as a permanent minority to Hindus unless they got their own Stan. And while we're referencing India, it won't surprise you that Pakistan is vastly more populous than the others—more populous than Russia, in fact—with almost twice as many citizens as the other six Stans combined. It's also the only Stan that doesn't speak a Persian or Turkic language; British colonists wanted this region to mix with the rest of British India, so they imposed Urdu, a close relation to Hindi, which is still the lingua franca.

Given all this, Pakistan doesn't belong with the others. It's also the only Stan with a coastline, a cricket team, and nuclear weapons. This keeps the weekends interesting.

AFRICA

DEMOCRATIC REPUBLIC OF THE CONGO:
THE GREAT AFRICAN WAR

*Every time there was a change of armed group, the first
thing they did was to immediately start digging for gold.*

—RESIDENT OF NORTHEASTERN D.R. CONGO
TO HUMAN RIGHTS WATCH, 2004

- Rwanda and Uganda v. Hutu extremists
- Rwanda and Uganda v. the guy they put in power after beating the Hutus
- Rwanda, Uganda, and Burundi v. D.R. Congo, Chad, Libya, Angola, Namibia, and Zimbabwe
- Rwanda v. Uganda
- Lendu v. Hema (proxy war for Rwanda v. Uganda)

ote: The awfulness here is orders of magnitude worse than most other entries. The following is grouped together not to minimize the horrors, but because they interlock. I implore you to learn more than this eeny paperback can offer.)

If you had to find the world's deadliest conflict since WWII on a globe, where would your finger land?

Southeast Asia during the Vietnam War era would have been my guess, where the death toll was maybe three and a half million over the course of fifteen years.

The recent Congolese Civil Wars (aka the Great African War, the

African World War, and unrepeatable names) caused at least 3.8 million deaths. In six years.

That's more than twice as many deaths as the United States has suffered in all of its wars in history.

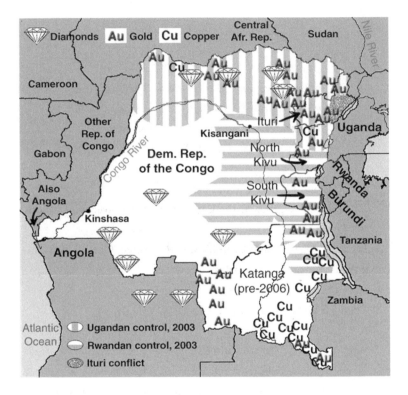

STARTING IN THE MIDDLE, AT THE BEGINNING

The Berlin Conference of 1884–85 (see "Western Sahara/Sahrawi Republic," p. 87) gave the region now called the Democratic Republic of Congo to King Leopold II of Belgium. Not to Belgium, mind you—to *Leopold,* personally, who now owned every rock, stick, and human life in the territory. Period. Unfortunately, Leopold was a total sociopath.

The new land's ironic name: the Congo Free State. Its first major new settlement: Leopoldville, of course. And the next twenty-four years were bad. The violence unleashed by Leopold's men rivals anything in history. Total losses? Maybe 10 million.

It took decades for all this to become public, but in 1908, Belgium's parliament took away Leopold's toy. When he died, he was so despised that Belgians reportedly booed his corpse.

The new colonial Belgian Congo was a big improvement, which is to say people's hands were no longer severed to meet government quotas. Finally, in the 1950s, a strengthening independence movement was led by Patrice Lumumba, a charismatic leftist. His rivals were Joseph Kasavubu, a conservative nationalist, plus a faction from the mineral-rich province of Katanga, a profit center for Belgian industry.

After independence in 1960, Lumumba became prime minister, but Kasavubu was elected president. Unfortunately, nobody—Belgian or Congolese—had prepared for the transition. On the sixth day, the army rebelled. On the twelfth day, Katanga seceded, supported by Belgian industrialists.

Desperate to hold things together and impatient with the UN, Lumumba asked for Soviet help. This didn't please the West. Pretty soon, a CIA-backed colonel named Joseph Mobutu seized power, suspended parliament, and sent the Russians home.

Kasavubu remained as president, but Lumumba was arrested and executed. (The CIA gets blamed, but a Belgian inquiry puts the blame squarely on Belgians and Katangans.) Lumumba remains the martyred hero of Congolese nationhood, invoked by leaders ever since, including Joseph Mobutu, who helped kill Lumumba to begin with.

UN and Congolese troops defeated the breakaway factions, but a new leftist revolt emerged in the east, led in part by one of Lumumba's old commanders, Laurent Kabila. This Simba ("lion" in Swahili) rebellion captured almost half of the nation's territory. Once this new uprising was again quelled by U.S. and Belgian troops, Kabila's faction retreated to an enclave near the Rwandan border, where they survived via farming, smuggling, and covert aid from China. Picture Robin Hood and his men, but with AK-47s and no moral center. Kabila became wealthy and invisible, but he'll return shortly.

Tired of instability, the CIA went full-on behind Joseph Mobutu, who seized absolute power for the next thirty-two years. Ditching symbols of Belgian colonialism, Mobutu changed *Congo* to *Zaire, Leopoldville* to *Kinshasa*, and *Joseph Mobutu* to *Mobutu Sese Seko Koko Ngbendu Wa Za Banga*. Good for him. Mobutu then proceeded with the psychotic-dictator thing, torturing and mass-killing opponents before large audiences while amassing a billion-dollar fortune as his country sank into poverty.

The CIA got their anti-Soviet state, Mobutu received over $1 billion in aid from the United States, and Western leaders unflinchingly shook Mobutu's bloody hand. Vice President Bush lauded Mobutu's "dedication to fairness and reason," and Ronald Reagan praised the mass murderer as "a voice of good sense and goodwill."

In 1994, Mobutu supported the Hutu extremists conducting genocide against Tutsis in Rwanda. In under four months, nearly a million Tutsis and moderate Hutus were slaughtered. But to understand Rwanda fully, we have to swing through Uganda next.

UGANDA

Uganda was colonized by the British, but the dominant Bugandan culture considered obedience a duty, so the Bugandan king became Britain's eager agent. This didn't please most non-Bugandans, so as independence approached in 1960, an activist named Milton Obote built an alliance from other ethnic groups. In 1962, Uganda entered nationhood with a Bugandan figurehead, King Freddie (honest), but with Obote holding the real power as prime minister. Soon, Obote and one of his commanders, Idi Amin, were accused of looting gold and ivory out of the Congo (a preview of the massive tragedy to come). Obote sacked King Freddie, suspended the constitution, and sent his army into parliament, who quickly decided Obote wasn't guilty after all.

Corruption and multifaceted ethnic fractures have been staples of Ugandan politics ever since. After Idi Amin overthrew Obote in 1971, · Obote set up a rebel force in Tanzania. Amin began torturing and killing opponents; he also lined up with Libya, the PLO, and the Soviets. The West severed trade. Amin severed heads. Life sucked.

Amin attacked Tanzania in 1978, but Obote, anti-Amin exiles, and the Tanzanian army were stronger. Amin fled to Saudi Arabia, leaving behind a body count of maybe 300,000.

Obote's second regime proved not much kinder than Amin's; *another* six-figure number of Ugandans were killed. But in 1985, Obote was overthrown, and soon a rebel leader named Yoweri Museveni was in charge. Museveni brought stability and diminished carnage. But war, unfortunately, never stopped. In Uganda's north, ethnic hostilities toward the new government facilitated the rise of a self-proclaimed Lord's Resistance Army, whose interpretation of the Christian Bible has condoned their child kidnappings, rape, and mutilations for twenty years and counting.

In Rwanda, meanwhile, Tutsis have viewed Museveni as a key ally. Since Tutsis in Uganda had been on the receiving end of Obote's hellfire, many had joined Museveni in overthrowing Obote. Museveni remained pro-Tutsi, later supporting the Rwandese Patriotic Front (RPF), a Tutsi group led by Museveni's head of intelligence, Paul Kagame, in its effort to take over Rwanda.

RWANDA

With fertile soil and a climate tempered by altitude, Rwanda (like its sister, Burundi) is one of the most densely populated bits of Africa.

THE DIFFERENCE BETWEEN TUTSI AND HUTU

In short: not all that much. Tutsis and Hutus have lived on the same land, spoken the same languages, intermarried, and sometimes had trouble telling each other apart for centuries. Genetically, they're indistinguishable. Y'know that episode of *Star Trek* where Frank Gorshin has half his face painted black, and some other guy has the other half painted black, and they *hate* each other? This is that.

Despite theories of different ethnic origins, it seems more likely that the particular Tutsis in charge when German colonists arrived had slightly more European features, so the Germans thought maybe that speck of whiteness made the Tutsis special. And we all know how well German racial theories worked out.

In any case, Tutsis had cattle, and Hutus didn't, but under 19th-century rules, a Hutu could become Tutsi just by gaining wealth. Still, Tutsis tended to marry other well-off Tutsis, just as rich people do in most societies. After a few generations, you'd have ingrained animosities. Genetics aren't necessary here; the French Revolution didn't have an ethnic component, but blood poured during the Reign of Terror. What matters: enough locals believed in the difference.

Imagine the population of New York City, without skyscrapers, spread thickly over a New Jersey–sized area. That's Rwanda.

Rwanda was originally colonized by the Germans, who found a society with a somewhat feudal structure in which a small minority of cattle-owning Tutsi people were lording it over a majority population of Hutus. After WWI, Rwanda became a Belgian protectorate. And we've already seen what brilliant colonists the Belgians were next door in the Congo.

The Belgians kept a bunch of Tutsis in charge, using them to enforce a regime of forced labor for the profit of European exporters. Tutsis also got education and privileges; Hutus didn't. Fast-forward a few decades, and hatred became seriously entrenched.

That social resentments ultimately resulted in megadeath is well-known. Thanks to *Hotel Rwanda* and after-the-fact tut-tutting, most Westerners are now aware of the 1994 butchery of about 800,000 Tutsis and moderate Hutus, about which the world was warned yet did less than nothing. (UN troops were actually pulled out *during* the slaughter.)

Thing is, the tragedy wasn't unprecedented, so the world could hardly plead surprise. In Burundi, more than 100,000 people were slaughtered in 1972, for example—only this time, it was the ruling-minority Tutsis killing Hutus. Thousands of Hutus fled into Rwanda. Hutu-Tutsi massacres (or vice versa) also reportedly occurred in Burundi or Rwanda in 1959, 1963–65, 1969, 1988, and 1993. The claim that nobody could have foreseen the Rwandan genocide is simply not credible.

Four years before 1994's genocide, the Uganda-based Tutsi RPF staged a surprise incursion into Rwanda. This was repelled by the Hutu government's army, but Paul Kagame—whose own family fled Rwanda during the 1959 strife—led the RPF into hiding and began staging commando raids across Rwanda's north. By 1993, the RPF was strong enough to threaten a move on Rwanda's capital.

Hutus responded by fleeing, spewing pure hatred for all things Tutsi, and/or stockpiling weapons. The UN's local commander warned that mass murder might be imminent.

In 1994, peace talks had made surprising progress, but the Hutu presidents of Rwanda and Burundi were both killed when their plane was shot down. Hutu extremists have usually been blamed, but a French judge recently implicated Kagame's Tutsi faction. Nothing has been proven either way. The aftermath, however, was unambiguous: Hutu machetes, Tutsi blood, global inaction. After 400,000 people were killed in less than a month, the UN mumbled that "acts of genocide" "may" have occurred.

Kagame's RPF finally rolled in from Uganda and Tanzania like the cavalry. To Kagame's credit, his new government refrained from revenge slaughter, but instead set up a Truth and Reconciliation process, decrying "Hutu" and "Tutsi" in favor of just "Rwandan." Although Kagame's government is still mostly Tutsi. Hmph.

In *Hotel Rwanda*, this is where survivors reunite, take comfort in one another's survival, and power-walk into the credits. In reality, however, the worst was yet to come.

TWO MILLION DEAD SO FAR; NOW THINGS GET *REALLY* BAD

About 2 million Hutus fled the country, fearing conflict, revenge massacres, and/or prosecution. Maybe a million landed in emergency shelters in Zaire (the former Congo) near the Rwandan border. These camps were ravaged by diarrhea, cholera, and more; fortunately, guilt-stricken Western countries poured aid into the region, saving tens of thousands of lives. Unfortunately, the camps also gave Hutu extremists a place to reorganize, eventually asserting contol over the incoming aid. Relief agencies were forced to begin pulling out.

With Hutus frequently raiding Rwanda, the Tutsis created a militia inside Zaire to respond. But in Zaire's capital, Mobutu supported the Hutu raids, so Rwanda and Uganda hooked up with Laurent Kabila (Mobutu's old enemy, the one whose men went all Sherwood Forest a few decades earlier) to ultimately move against Mobutu. Kabila, backed by Rwanda and Uganda, pushed all the way into Kinshasa, killing uncounted thousands en route. In 1997, Kabila sacked Mobutu, became president, and ditched *Zaire* for the *Democratic Republic of the Congo.* However, to many Congolese, Kabila seemed a puppet of Rwanda, Uganda, and the Tutsis he rode in on. For Kabila, retaining power meant cutting ties to his patrons, which he tried in 1998. Bad move.

Like a football team with one good play, Uganda, Rwanda, and kid brother Burundi immediately began arming *another* batch of Congolese Tutsis to overthrow the guy they had just installed. In response, Kabila convinced several neighbors to come to his aid, mostly from self-interest. Zimbabwe's Robert Mugabe (see "Zimbabwe," p. 83) signed huge mining deals with Kabila, as did the president of Namibia. Angola, meanwhile, was fighting rebels based in southern Congo, who financed themselves with blood diamonds (see "Liberia, Sierra Leone, and Côte d'Ivoire," p. 74, for similar events). Angola was happy to send in troops.

In the ensuing four years, neither side was strong enough to secure even its own territory; "strategy" often amounted to protecting specific resources. Given endemic poverty, the simplest way to keep financing the battle was to yank as many goodies out of the ground as possible, hustle the stuff to a middleman, and keep rolling. Soon, profiteering became the war's dominant feature. According to the UN, the Rwandan army yanked a quarter of a billion dollars out of the ground just in 1999 and 2000. The International Court of Justice deemed Uganda guilty of eventually looting billions.

The combatants weren't the only ones making bank. Like

Leopold a century earlier, numerous corporations—from Africa, Europe, and the Americas—didn't care where the resources came from or what weapons were involved. I've sketched the rough distribution of three lucrative commodities—diamonds, gold, and copper—as best as I'm able, but there simply isn't room for all the valuables. One example: North and South Kivu contain 75 percent of the world's supply of an ore containing a rare metal used in electronic capacitors. Your cell phone and the laptop I'm writing this on probably contain tiny bits of the eastern Congo. In 2000, this ore sold for $300 per pound. The local per capita annual income was about $200. Put that stuff in the ground—plus gold, diamonds, silver, etc.—then add poverty, AK-47s, and generations of hatred. Stir.

A 1999 peace deal acknowledged the standoff, but the killing didn't stop. Soon, Uganda and Rwanda split over control of Kisangani, a town near several gold and diamond mines. The war now had *three* major factions, none of whom could win, but all of whom had big financial incentive to keep playing. Finally, the UN got seriously involved, and while it's easy to criticize the slow progress that followed, without the blue hats, things would have been way worse.

The broader war formally ended in 2003 for multiple reasons: Western pressure on Rwanda and Uganda, UN intervention, South African peace talks, a drop in the export price of key commodities (the Western tech collapse may even have helped), and sheer damn fatigue.

An appalling sideshow: the conflict in Ituri, where Lendu and Hema people have traded the stinkeye for a century. Neither side was well-armed until the last decade, when the Hema started receiving Ugandan arms while Lendus got guns from Rwanda. The alliances have since shifted, but all told, tens of thousands have been killed. Fortunately, as this goes to print, it appears all involved may be laying down their weapons. Let's hope.

After all this, it would be bizarre indeed to end with a bright note.

One exists: the 2003 deal, despite periodic violations, has held so far. In 2006, reasonable national elections were held under a revamped constitution, and the results didn't lead directly to mass murder. So that's new. The new president: Joseph Kabila, son of Laurent Kabila. Among young Joe's closest advisors: widely denounced war profiteers. So that's not new. Neither are violent flare-ups. By the time you read this, peace may well have ended.

Even if it hasn't, four years later, the war continues to take a cruel toll. According to the UN, about 1,200 people—more than half of them children—continue to die each day from war-related diseases and hunger. That would be over 400,000 more deaths this year, even if all violence ceases.

How bad was the Great African War? If my math isn't screwy, in 2007, more people may die from its aftermath than from all other active wars in the world, combined.

SUDAN

- Khartoum v. Southern Sudan and anything that moves, peace deal 2005
- Khartoum v. Eastern Front, peace deal 2006
- Khartoum v. Darfur rebels and anything that moves, continuing

Sudan is hardly even a functional country; during its fifty-one years of independence, Sudan has engaged in civil wars for forty. And counting.

Sudan is huge—about as big as the U.S. east of Chicago—and so contains several distinct geographies, chiefly: (a) an arid, Arab, Muslim north, culturally akin to nearby Egypt, and (b) a swampier south, more like Kenya and Uganda, populated by East African cultures practicing mixtures of Christian and animist traditions.

Sudan's boundaries are mostly the work of British colonists, who weren't exactly detail oriented. (To this day, corners of the Egyptian and Kenyan borders have never really been resolved, although this is a teeny stress compared to everything else.) British colonists focused almost entirely on the north, leaving the rural south undeveloped and culturally separate. This made sense: Egypt was the regional power, and the north had all the coastline plus two-thirds of the population. Colonialism is like anything else in real estate: location, location, location.

Still, after WWII, the UK handed independence to all of Sudan, theoretically united under one government in Khartoum. Theoretically. In reality, civil war began before independence even began. Cumulative death toll: more than 2 million, mostly southerners.

The war paused in 1972, when the north granted the south a degree of autonomy. Soon thereafter, oil exploration began in earnest, and 80 percent of the oil was found in the south. Not surprisingly, in 1983, Khartoum decided to screw southern autonomy, mandate the Arabic language, and institute Islamic Sharia law everywhere. In a word: *gimme*.

To enforce its claim to the south, Khartoum sponsored militias that engaged in the torture and murder of civilians, the enslavement of women and children, and the use of rape as a weapon. In 1989, Gen. Omar Al-Bashir, who had led numerous attacks against southern rebels, seized power. Al-Bashir has been a world-class bad guy ever since, siding with Saddam Hussein in the 1991 Gulf War, hosting Osama Bin Laden in his salad days, and helping to create a 1998 famine by wiping out an entire crop for military reasons.

Along the way, Al-Bashir has also abolished Sudan's parliament and named himself prime minister, president, chief of state, and defense minister. I haven't checked, but he's probably also the sole judge and winner of each year's *Sudanese Idol*.

Most of the country remained bone-grindingly poor, but thanks to the oil, Khartoum boomed. However, international condemnation threatened the economy, so north/south peace talks began in 2002. That's when two *other* rebel groups demanded autonomy and shares of the oil pie. In the northeast, non-Arab Beja and Rashaida rebels (the "Eastern Front") threatened to attack their end of the pipeline. Khartoum responded, as in the south, by arming local Arab militias to respond violently, but in 2006, a truce granted the Eastern Front increased money and power.

In the south, where rebellion also posed a threat to the oil infrastructure, civil war ended in 2005 with a deal promising six years of autonomy, an eventual independence vote, and a 50-50 oil money split. (That said, given South Sudan's desire for independence, all hell should reboot before long. One hint: the south, despite urgent poverty, spends about half its income on its military.)

That leaves Darfur, where ethnic Fur and Masalit rebels similarly took up arms. Surprisingly, the rebels actually won a few minor victories until Khartoum, perhaps unimpeded by major oil-security concerns, responded with overwhelming brutality against the entire region, rebels and civilians alike.

Since 2003, Khartoum's Arab militia in Darfur, the Janjaweed ("devils on horseback"), have engaged in savagery against non-Arabs akin to that once practiced in South Sudan, augmented by frequent support from Sudanese aircraft. By 2004, more than 100,000 civilians in Darfur had been killed, and more than 400 villages had been destroyed. Numerous world leaders, including both U.S. presidential candidates, used the term *genocide.*

Sadly, this high-profile U.S. interest largely dissolved after the political campaign. Despite the ongoing crisis—with a death toll now twice (and perhaps four times) that of 2004—the U.S. Agency for International Development's website actually indicates that the conflict is *over,* trumpeting a May 2006 agreement that actually failed within days. Even more absurdly, the 2006 edition of the State Department annual "Country Report on Terrorism" describes Sudan's government as both a "state sponsor" of terrorism and a "strong partner in the War on Terror"—both on the *very same page.* Why? The *Los Angeles Times* later reported that the Bush administration has secretly worked with the Sudanese government to gather intelligence on both Iraq and Somalia. Perhaps not surprisingly, while the White House has recently announced a new round of economic sanctions, Sudan's key oil exports reportedly remain largely untouched.

That oil money buys a lot of guns. A 2005 UN arms embargo prohibits the sale of weapons directly into the conflict, but it technically allows sales to Khartoum as long as everyone *says* the guns aren't headed to Darfur. Khartoum can simply claim they're arming in self-defense while supporting the Janjaweed as a deniable proxy.

And so it goes. In recent months, the Janjaweed have followed fleeing refugees into neighboring Chad, where even some Chadians have joined in the killing. In February 2007, the UN High Commissioner for Refugees warned of another Rwanda in the making.

Will anyone respond this time? At this writing, Sudan's dictator refuses to allow UN troops into the country; the only peacekeepers on the scene are from the African Union, with seven thousand men to cover an area the size of Spain. The U.S. ability to intervene is severely compromised by other wars; China—Sudan's biggest oil investor—

will veto any UN sanctions; and no government—not from the West, Mideast, or Far East—is really pushing very hard to change anything.

More than two million people have been forced from their homes.

The ethnic cleansing continues.

UPDATE: The International Criminal Court has issued a forty-two-count war-crimes indictment against Ahmad Harun, a Sudanese government official accused of coordinating numerous attacks on civilians. Harun should not be hard to locate. He's currently the Minister for Humanitarian Affairs.

SOMALIA

- Violent clan rivalries
- Islamists v. warlords, Ethiopians, and the U.S.
- Pirates up the wazoo

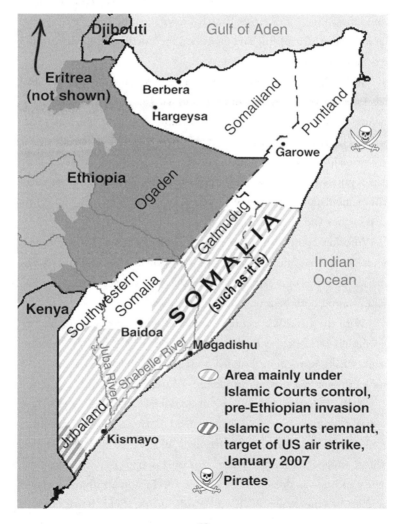

omalia existed as a functioning nation for only thirty
years, an era that ended more than fifteen years ago. The current state of Somalia is that there isn't one, exactly.

In the 19th century, the Horn of Africa (modern Ethiopia, Eritrea, Djibouti, and Somalia) was a modest prize to European
colonists, offering few resources but some control over Red Sea shipping lanes. (See "Western Sahara/Sahrawi Republic," p. 87, for the
Scramble for Africa.) England glommed the north, while Italy got the
less-valuable south.

WWII left both halves of Somalia under Allied control. These had
developed large differences during colonial rule, but nationalists and
former colonial powers decided on a unified Somalia anyway. Independence came in 1960, with fractures following almost instantly.

Somali culture also challenges any centralized government, since
clan loyalties (there are a half-dozen major affiliations) often seem to
trump any national identity. With guns if necessary. Somalis apparently
have serious family values.

Another complication was the Allies' decision to hand Ogaden,
whose people are mostly Somali-speaking Muslims considered by Somalis as distant clan members, to Ethiopia. Ogaden separatism and Somali invasion both became likely developments.

With the Cold War raging, Somalis also had to decide if their rifles should be marked with Roman characters or Cyrillic. Fresh mem-
ories of European colonialism led most Somalis to lean Red, especially
since Ethiopia was playing for the pro-Western Blue team.

A 1969 coup ended all hope of democracy, however, replacing it
with the dictatorship of Mohamed Siad Barre, Somalia's sole ruler
until the fall of centralized government in 1991. Siad Barre ran your
typical thugocracy: secret police, torture, disappearances, etc., with
favors and power doled out by clan. After Ethiopia suffered a power
vacuum in the wake of its dictator's death, Siad Barre invaded

Ogaden. However, Moscow considered Ethiopia's replacement dictator, Mengistu Haile Mariam, a promising ally, and Ethiopia was the bigger catch. Moscow switched sides, Somalia was forced to retreat, and Mengistu's Red Terror went on to kill at least half a million Ethiopians. (He's a free man, unfortunately, advising Robert Mugabe; see "Zimbabwe," p. 83.)

Naturally, the U.S. switched the other way, backing Siad Barre despite his brutal one-party rule. Why? To oppose the Soviets, *silly.* Berbera was also a useful port, what with the oil tankers whizzing by. The U.S. gave Berbera the longest airstrip in Africa, and the base later became part of U.S. deployment operations for the first Gulf War.

By then, Siad Barre was losing his grip. Given his inability to grab Ogaden, plus drought and hunger made worse by an unworkable economic system, Siad Barre increasingly relied on his Red Beret death squad, slaughtering civilians over bloodlines and destroying reservoirs in desert areas to kill whole villages via mass dehydration.

By 1991, Siad Barre's regime dissolved in chaotic revolt, and the former British Somaliland, hundreds of miles to the north, decided *screw this* and seceded. Somaliland has remained relatively quiet—by Somali standards—ever since, building a stable (if unrecognized) government in Hargeysa directly upon existing clan social structures.

While Mogadishu descended into *Black Hawk Down,* other chunks of the country have also asserted some level of autonomy. Jubaland, south of the Juba river, jumped in 1998, soon rivaled by the Juba Valley Alliance (JVA) and another self-declared state, Southwestern Somalia. Jubaland was still the most fun to say. Puntland bailed about the same time, soon squabbling with Somaliland over their boundary. Incidentally, Puntland provides no coastal patrols near the strategic Horn, so that's world-class pirate territory.

Believe it or not, these hassles have been handled fairly peaceably—by Somali standards—thanks to a 2000 conference in Djibouti that brought together bitter factions and led to the Transitional Federal Government (TFG), the closest thing Somalia has to, well, *that*. Plenty of factions aren't on board, of course. It took six years before the TFG could even convene inside Somalia, and instead of Mogadishu, it was in a converted warehouse in Baidoa.

During the last few years, meanwhile, many warlords—who, despite the term, are sometimes just guys who have military control over an area but aren't aggressively trying to kill everybody else—have gone Michael Corleone, converting their militias into profitable security for hire. Once territories are marked, some stability exists, so over the last few years, diverse capitalist enterprises have arisen.

At the same time, the rule of law (such as it is) has been enforced by Islamic courts. The whole country is Muslim—don't even bring up other religions—so Sharia law was one of the few structures people could agree on, especially in madhouses like Mogadishu. The courts needed militias to enforce their rulings, so before long they, too, were running a protection racket, with local businesses paying the Islamic court cops to keep their streets clean. Pretty soon, the courts built alliances, and by 2006, you've got the Islamic Courts Union (ICU), armed to the teeth and aggressively asserting power.

The CIA thought the ICU was probably harboring Al-Qaeda guys, something the ICU consistently denied. Soon, like clockwork, a secular union of anti-ICU warlords popped up, the Alliance for the Restoration of Peace and Counter-Terrorism, widely rumored to receive heavy CIA financing. However, the Islamists kicked warlord ass, driving them clear out of Mogadishu.

With the warlords in retreat, the ICU pressed its advantage; within months, it gained control over almost the entire country south of Puntland. (The autonomous area of Galmudug was declared partly in defiance.) For better or worse, things were at least stable. For a good twenty minutes or so.

In the fall of 2006, however, Ethiopia sent thousands of troops in support of the warehouse government and the warlord alliance. The Islamic Courts, meanwhile, reportedly received backing from Eritrea, a longtime adversary of Ethiopia. Next came Ethiopian tanks and helicopters, assisted (to an extent just surfacing) by U.S. intelligence and special forces. By the end of the year, the ICU was forced to abandon Mogadishu and flee to the southernmost corner of Jubaland, into the hills, and over the Kenyan border.

Unsatisfied, the United States decided there were Al-Qaeda big shots to hit, so in January 2007, U.S. helicopters zipped in and blew up some people from the air. Early reports indicate that dozens have been killed, although it's not clear if attacks actually hit their stated targets. In any case, the ICU's ferocity united several competing factions, and the Transitional Federal Government finally seated itself in Mogadishu for the first time. Things were at least stable. For another twenty minutes or so.

At this writing, much of Mogadishu has again been pummeled by shelling and firefights between supporters and opponents of the Ethiopian-backed TFG, which is certainly putting the "Transitional" part of its name to good use. More than 300,000 people have again fled from their homes.

Sadly, I cannot imagine things will have quieted much when you read this. Even if you've just found a dog-eared copy that your dad used to own.

LIBERIA, SIERRA LEONE, AND CÔTE D'IVOIRE:
BLOOD DIAMOND LAND

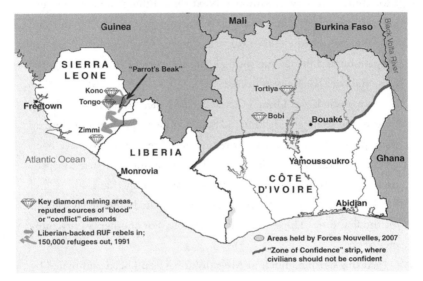

LIBERIA

- Multiple undemocratic governments and rebellions; now a shaky democracy
- Support for RUF rebellion in Sierra Leone

L iberia was founded in 1817 so American blacks could "return" to Africa. Considering they'd been yanked from cultures all over West Africa, this was racist on its face, but compared to slavery, this was also progress.

Unfortunately, Liberia resembled most other colonies. The colonists ("Americos") had little in common with the locals; after independence in 1847, Americos were a small percentage of the population but held all the political power. Ironically, rubber plantations made swaths of Liberia mildly resemble the antebellum U.S. south. Some Africans were even later sold to other colonists as—yes—*slaves.* After WWII, Liberia finally allowed everyone to vote, tampering with results instead. Western investment poured in, improving life in the capital but not for the rural majority. You can guess what follows: inequality, protests, and repression.

Boom, 1980: Samuel Doe, an army sergeant from the repressed Krahn ethnic group, seized power, murdered his rivals, and doled out advantage to fellow Krahns. But since Doe was anticommunist, the U.S. supported his regime, what with Liberia being the only thing keeping the Soviets from seizing . . . um . . . southern Guinea, maybe.

The Wrath of Krahn brought inevitable backlash. In 1989, non-Krahns organized around Charles Taylor, a former embezzler with Libyan military training whose Côte d'Ivoire–based uprising nearly seized power. However, a splinter faction run by one of his former commanders, Prince Johnson, got to Monrovia first.

Johnson's rebels captured Samuel Doe, tortured him to death, and videotaped the event for posterity. Johnson reportedly presided over Doe's mutilation while sitting at a desk, wearing a hand-grenade necklace, quaffing a Budweiser, and being fanned by a young woman. After Johnson ordered Doe's ears cut off, the tape ends, and thank you sweet Jesus. Supposedly, Johnson then forced Doe to eat one of his own ears.

Next time anyone claims that U.S. politicians play hardball, I will disagree.

Prince Johnson is now a Pentecostal minister. I bet his collection plate is always full.

However, to Johnson's surprise, torture didn't bring peace. *Go fig-ure.* Fighting flared among more than a half-dozen groups, often using child fighters armed to the teeth. Liberia's population and size are comparable with Mississippi; imagine that when you realize that more than 200,000 people eventually died.

Meanwhile, one of Taylor's compatriots, Foday Sankoh, started a civil war next door in Sierra Leone. (See below.) Sankoh's Revolutionary United Front (RUF) seized key diamond mines, sending the booty into Liberia in exchange for fresh weaponry. Exporting these "blood" diamonds made Taylor rich. The UN later found that twice as many "Liberian" diamonds entered Europe as Liberia's own mines could generate.

Back in Liberia, a hinky election took place in 1997. Taylor won easily, mostly because people were afraid that if they didn't vote for him, he'd start another war. One slogan: "He killed my ma, he killed my pa . . . but *I* will vote for him." Catchy.

Things then sucked. Unemployment hit 80 percent while life expectancy dropped to forty. Most of the money Taylor's government got went either into his own pocket or into seizing more diamonds next door, which were typically smuggled out via Côte d'Ivoire.

Taylor also benefited from increasingly granting Liberian registries to international ships. Under such flags of convenience, the ship's owner pays for the legal right to pretend to be Liberian, avoiding First World regulations and fees. (Numerous developing countries now engage in this practice, including Bolivia and Mongolia, both of which are landlocked.) In Taylor's era, Liberian-registered cruise ships therefore indirectly subsidized mass murder.

Taylor's brutality led to rebellion from the anti–Taylor Liberians United for Reconciliation and Democracy (LURD, which is at least fun to say). LURD committed atrocities, too, while seizing much of Liberia's north. Liberia's south was captured by the Movement for Democracy in Liberia (MODEL), mostly Krahns backed by Côte d'Ivoire. Soon, Taylor controlled only the capital. Then LURD cut off his supply of food and fuel. Game over. Taylor resigned, leaving the country to LURD, MODEL, and vice president Blah. (That's not just filler. His name was really Moses Blah.)

Charles Taylor is now in The Hague, facing war crimes prosecution.

Back in Liberia, peacekeepers have disbanded the army and held the first real democratic elections in history. The new president is Ellen Johnson-Sirleaf, a former Citibank economist from Harvard who opposed both Doe and Taylor when it counted. Unfortunately, the legislature includes several of Taylor's allies who wouldn't mind seeing the new president dead. Also, the disbanded army was promised they'd be paid for their troubles. They haven't been. And Prince Johnson speaks for them in Monrovia.

One hopes that Johnson never quite gets the president's ear.

SIERRA LEONE

- RUF v. dictatorship, civilians, mercenaries, and the world

During the U.S. Revolutionary War, the British offered freedom to any American slave who fought on their side. Afterward, many were sent to Sierra Leone. As in Liberia, disease and hostility decimated the settlers, but the newcomers' connections helped them impose minority rule.

Unlike Liberia, however, Sierra Leone's economy grew around stripping the land of resources. In 1935, the South African De Beers company (see "Zimbabwe," p. 83) established a monopoly that solidified the country's economic structure.

When the colony gained independence in 1961, the ruling Sierra Leone Peoples Party (SLPP) was dominated by the largest ethnic group, the Mende. (Ever see *Amistad*? Those guys were Mende.) The SLPP did okay until its leader died and his brother took over. If you've seen *The Godfather*, this was like Fredo taking over the family.

The SLPP's main rival was the All People's Congress (APC), led by Siaka Stevens, a non-Mende who rose to power in 1967 by pushing ethnic tension. Stevens eventually held power through violence and corruption until the age of eighty. Stevens's successor, however, was another Fredo, and his regime dissolved into an orgy of backroom deals. Virtually every state apparatus began to fail, and by 1991, the country was short on food and electricity, but long on resentment and weaponry.

That's when Liberia's Charles Taylor decided his buddy Foday Sankoh should roll in, seize power, and grab a boatload of diamonds. Sankoh's Revolutionary United Front (RUF) terrorized the crap out of countless victims, with decapitations, heads on sticks, severed limbs, and anything else you want to keep yourself up at night imagining.

Those allowed to live were often forced into picking and shoveling for diamonds. (This arduous labor is quaintly called *artisanal,* as if people are baking bread.) The RUF also grabbed thousands of children, shoved guns in their hands and drugs in their bloodstream, and turned them into fighters.

At least 75,000 people died as the conflict developed. In the northeast, hundreds of thousands were forced to flee into the "Parrot's Beak" of Guinea, where they were surrounded on three sides by bad guys and on the fourth by an unwelcoming Guinean army. The desperation is visible in satellite photos: before the war, the Parrot's Beak was lush countryside, but after, it was stripped nearly bare.

By 1995, the RUF controlled almost all of Sierra Leone and had the capital surrounded. The "developed" world did squat—the UN and the West didn't show up until 1999, after tens of thousands were dead, and 2 million had fled—so in desperation, Sierra Leone appealed to Executive Outcomes, a private firm made up mostly of apartheid-era South African soldiers turned machine-guns-for-hire. (Such organizations also offer private armies to oil companies, banks, and other multinationals doing business in angry parts of the world.) Sure enough, Executive Outcomes did the Rambo thing and kicked drug-addled child-soldier war-criminal ass.

The operation was partly bankrolled by foreign mining investors who cut in Executive Outcomes for a percentage, but a few years later, Sierra Leone still owed $23 million to Executive Outcomes. In a twist straight from a bad summer movie, two random guys in Michigan had *another* company called Executive Outcomes, and Sierra Leone accidentally contacted *them*. The Michigan dudes said, "Sure! We'll take $23 million!" and then probably called every girl they'd ever met. They're going to jail now.

The military held surprisingly free elections in 1996, but peace talks failed, since the RUF version of disarmament was much too literal. Pro-RUF army officers then kick-started a new war with an assault on Freetown called Operation No Living Thing, which was appallingly well-named. This time the RUF was repelled by West African peace-keeping forces. Finally, in 1999, after the near-destruction of Freetown, a peace accord was signed in Togo; UN forces have since disarmed more than 75,000 men, keeping peace with only minor incident.

Meanwhile, the diamond industry met in Kimberley, South Africa, to create a profit-protecting way to certify a stone's origin, since nobody wants Westerners to associate diamonds with horror. (Never mind that De Beers profited from apartheid prison labor for decades.) Ultimately, the Kimberley Process promises to solve everything through voluntary compliance. Self-enforced. With a straight face.

CÔTE D'IVOIRE

- "Ivoirité" south v. northern Forces Nouvelles

Soon after Côte d'Ivoire gained independence from France in 1960, the first president, Félix Houphouët-Boigny, won Western acclaim as a beacon of democracy. Never mind that opposing him in elections was illegal, and he ruled as president-for-life until his own prostate gland finally ended his term in 1993. (*Houphouët,* incidentally, is pronounced "oofway," like "woof" in pig Latin. *Boigny* is a Baoulé suffix meaning "strong"; Oofway modestly affixed it to his own name.)

Oofway the Great also lined his own pockets with government funds, dumped his wife for a hottie young enough to be his daughter, and relocated the capital from Abidjan, the country's major trading port, to Yamoussoukro, the remote village where he was born. Imagine Clinton moving the White House to Hope, Arkansas, and you get the lunacy. So why all the praise for his integrity and wisdom?

Simple: for decades, Côte d'Ivoire was the most prosperous spot in West Africa. Oofway's grip provided enough stability that multinationals felt confident investing, and his larceny was small enough that regular folks did OK, minimizing dissent. Since the government rarely resorted to violence, the shock-baton budget could be spent instead on infrastructure, attracting more investment. Plus, when Oofway the Ategray quelled periodic riots, coups, and demonstrations, he did so without mass murder. So Oofwayland wasn't a democracy, but it wasn't horrible, either, for the first twenty years.

Unfortunately, the Oof got cocky. In the 1970s, when commodity prices were high, he borrowed heavily to invest in state projects, hoping to stimulate further growth. When coffee and cocoa prices unexpectedly dove, Côte d'Ivoire quickly went from Africa's rich kid to crippling debitude. Eventually, Oofway grew unhinged. His last project involved spending $300 million—in a poor country—to celebrate himself with the largest church on earth.

Oofalissimo Francisco Franco died in 1993, leaving power to Henri Bédié, whose rule was Dictator 101. His worst move was necessitating *Ivoirité*—true-blue Ivorianism—as a prerequisite for office, claiming that southern Ivorians, mostly Christian, are the only "real" Ivorians, while Muslim northerners are not. Since Côte d'Ivoire is a French colonial invention, and virtually every ethnic group around migrated from somewhere else, Ivoirité is absurd. But it gives people someone to blame, so it caught on. Houphouët looks positively Boigny by comparison.

Bédié's regime got caught repeatedly with its hand in the national cookie jar; by 1997, the country was bankrupt. International lenders, other governments, and everyone who wasn't Bédié started grokking his suckitude. In 1999, Bédié was overthrown by Robert Guéï. This is one of the few coups ever staged by someone named Bob. Bob promised that he wouldn't run for office. Then he ran for office. Bob insisted the elections would be fair. Then Bob cranked up the Ivoirité crap, disqualifying several opposition candidates, and his soldiers murdered opposition activists. After all the chicanery, the election was held . . . and Bob still lost. True to form, Bob refused to leave until the new president's guys ran him out.

The new boss was a former history professor named Laurent Gbagbo, whose supporters ("Young Patriots") beat the crap out of immigrants in the capital, especially people from Burkina Faso ("Burkinabes"), the country's largest minority. Northern Côte d'Ivoire has at least 3 million Burkinabes, so the "foreigner" perception had legs. With hate amped by hardship and cynical politicians, the country was becoming a tinderbox.

In 2002, Gbagbo tried to disarm Muslim and Burkinabe sections of the army to consolidate his power. The soldiers protested, which grew into a larger rebellion. Pretty soon, anti-Ivoirité rebels (the *Forces Nouvelles,* "New Forces") held the north (not to mention its diamond mines) and the pro-Ivoirité government controlled the south. However, since the "Zone of Confidence" was ruled by neither side, it was hardly safe.

Before long, a government death squad (the "Squadron of Death," creatively enough) started killing opposition leaders and squelching dissent. Thousands have died; more than a million have fled to Mali, Ghana, and other neighbors.

France brokered a power-sharing deal in 2003, but it fell apart when Gbagbo had some opponents killed. International pressure led to another peace deal in 2005, but Gbagbo hyped the race card enough to keep the country too messy to hold elections.

While six digits' worth of human beings remained in refugee camps ("welcome centers") and innocent people continued to die violently, elections were postponed until 2006 . . . and then 2007 . . . and it's still unclear if they'll ever take place. A peace deal was signed shortly before press time, elevating rebel leader Guillaume Soro to the role of prime minister (Gbagbo remains president) and promising reunification, peace, and elections . . . maybe in 2008. Exciting, except Soro's powers are undefined, numerous previous accords have accomplished little, and both sides seem to have more to gain from the status quo. Healthy skepticism is warranted; days after Gbagbo declared that the war was "over," the international aid group Médecins Sans Frontières reported a rapid increase in violence.

Given that two de facto states already exist, the original was a colonial fiction, and the Confidence Zone border has been stable, a split seems the only sane solution. However, the New Forces have rejected the notion. Why? No idea. But while the rebels deny any diamond smuggling, the UN pegs the illicit diamond trade at about $23 million annually. The New Forces' reluctance toward change may not be so odd.

One bright final note: a temporary cease-fire was arranged for the 2006 soccer World Cup, during which the country watched and participated as one. The national team, Les Éléphants, included northerners and southerners who played together easily.

It was a sad day when Côte d'Ivoire was eliminated. If the team had kept winning, the conflict might have been suspended for weeks.

Time to go back to war.

ZIMBABWE

- Robert Mugabe and his police state v. anyone who isn't Robert Mugabe

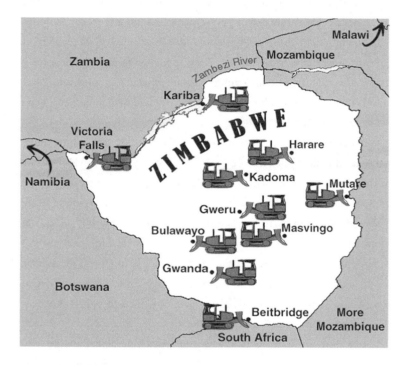

Can one man destroy a nation? Robert Mugabe is doing his best.

In the 19th century, the region was dominated by diamond tycoon Cecil Rhodes, head of the British South Africa Company, which (a) made its own laws, (b) had its own army, and therefore (c) convinced many African rulers to hand over their mineral rights.

Pretty soon, Cecil's chunk of Africa—modestly named "Rhode-sia"—was 50 percent larger than the UK. Donald Trump couldn't carry this guy's dry cleaning.

Rhodes fathered both the De Beers diamond empire and the introduction of the machine gun into African warfare. These were not coincidental. Cecil was also a spectacular racist and imperialist; Rhodes Scholarships stem from his wish to create a society of Anglo-Saxon elites to unify the world—*all of it,* Africa, Asia, your guest bathroom—under UK rule. Even *that* wouldn't have sufficed. Actual quote: "If I could, I would annex other planets." If Cecil had owned rockets, Mars would play cricket.

Brutality has been constant here, sadly. In 1930, the white rulers made it difficult for blacks to own land, reducing many to cheap labor in their own country. Black nationalist groups gathered steam for the next several decades. Eventually, the white government responded by outlawing dissident parties, apparently not noticing that they were outnumbered twenty to one. Full-on guerrilla war kicked in. The government drafted every white male, imported U.S. mercenaries whose screws had been loosened in Vietnam, and even released anthrax in rebel areas, causing thousands of innocent civilians to get freakin' *anthrax*. And still the rebellion continued.

But decolonialization in the rest of Africa isolated the minority government. So: the bargaining table. Eventually, independent Zimbabwe held real elections in 1980 amid international fanfare. This radiant new democracy with vast mineral and agricultural resources—the "breadbasket of Africa"—might finally live in peace.

Unfortunately, the first prime minister, Robert Mugabe—who looks and rules like a cross between Steve Urkel and Kim Jong-Il—took office amid charges of electoral intimidation. Welcome to the rest of the story.

Before resistance even began, Mugabe created a loyal anti-dissident cadre called the Fifth Brigade. Soon, when Mugabe's rivals rebelled in the farmlands of Matabeleland, Mugabe gave the Fifth Brigade its first big project. At least two thousand civilians were killed; most were innocent. Many were literally forced to dig their own graves. "We don't differentiate," Mugabe explained. "We can't tell who is a dissident and who is not." Saddam was hung for something similar.

Fast-forward: corruption, theft from the treasury, Mugabe making himself sole head of government, the good land getting handed out to his cronies . . . yadda, yadda, yadda . . .

In 1997, some of Mugabe's old compatriots demonstrated over still living in poverty, more than twenty years after they had supported his rise to power. Mugabe had never addressed the conditions of 1930—white ownership of farms, with blacks forced into cities and rural "tribal reserves"—so his army suddenly began seizing land owned by white farmers and redistributing it to his supporters. However, Mugabe's cronies weren't remotely trained or equipped, and the country was already in the middle of a terrible drought. At one stroke, Mugabe shut down his own country's food supply, creating famine. Two-thirds of Zimbabwe faced severe food shortages; half remains chronically undernourished even now. Mugabe's government, taking advantage, still uses food as a weapon, channeling relief aid away from opponents.

Onward: torture of opponents, secret police, youth cadres trained to act as militant pro-Mugabe brigades . . . Still, opposition has grown, particularly among the urban poor, who voted against Mugabe in the rigged 2005 elections. Mugabe responded to this feeble dissent with Operation Murambatsvina ("Getting Rid of the Fifth"), wiping out the urban shanties where his opposition lived: (a) bulldozer meets tin shack, (b) no more tin shack, and (c) no place else for the people who lived there. "Zimbabwe's Tsunami" wrecked the livelihoods of 700,000 people and screwed up millions of lives.

Police have also crushed large chunks of what passes for

Zimbabwe's middle class—informal tailors, plumbers, and tradespeople. Several suburbs of Harare now *no longer exist,* although Mugabe built a few replacement shacks without electricity or plumbing. This was "Operation Better Living."

Criticism of Mugabe remains illegal, and arrests come in waves, followed by beatings, torture, and killings. Police recently stopped a peaceful march in Harare, ordered five hundred people to sit down, and then beat them savagely—one at a time. At this writing, leading opposition figures are frequently pummeled.

Hundreds of thousands of people just want to escape. South Africa has responded by stationing troops on its border. Botswana is building a 300-mile electric fence. Great.

Scoreboard: Zimbabwe now has the world's worst life expectancy. Ten years ago, female life expectancy was sixty-three. Now it's thirty-four. Unemployment hovers around 80 percent, and Zimbabwe also has the planet's worst inflation, which recently reached 3,731 percent. In 1980, its dollar was worth more than the U.S. dollar; considering revaluations, the exchange rate is now over 250,000 to one.

In 2006, Zimbabwe had to delay printing more money because they couldn't afford the paper.

Zimbabwe is last in the world alphabetically; thanks to Mugabe, it may soon be last in everything else.

WESTERN SAHARA/SAHRAWI REPUBLIC

- Sahrawi exiles supported by Algeria v. Morocco and its colonists

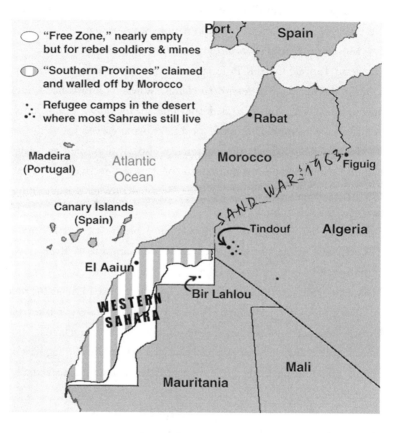

"Free Zone," nearly empty but for rebel soldiers & mines

"Southern Provinces" claimed and walled off by Morocco

Refugee camps in the desert where most Sahrawis still live

Port.

Spain

Madeira (Portugal)

Atlantic Ocean

Morocco

Rabat

SAND WAR 1963

Figuig

Canary Islands (Spain)

Tindouf

Algeria

El Aaiun

WESTERN SAHARA

Bir Lahlou

Mauritania

Mali

hether Western Sahara is an actual country depends on whom you ask.

In many Arab countries, this whole deal counts as Morocco. In South Africa, East Timor, and other post-colonial spots, it's the Sahrawi Arab Democratic Republic. In First World countries, it's the UN's mess. At the UN, it's up to the Sahrawis. But most

Sahrawis don't live here anymore, and it's not even clear who should count.

Let's back up—all the way to 1884 Berlin, in fact, where fourteen colonial powers began slicing up Africa like cake at a children's party. No representatives from any African nations were present.

Most European powers already had fingermarks in the frosting—France in Tunisia, the UK in Egypt, etc.—so the meeting was largely about codifying these as territorial claims. Where colonists had boots on the ground, land was handed out. This meant drawing big, nutty boundaries with no regard to the local folks being carved up.

In its defense, the Berlin conference also (a) abolished the slave trade on paper, which was great news for Africans enslaved on paper, and (b) established "peace," meaning colonial powers not shooting *each other* while conquering.

Meanwhile, Morocco, which had once hubbed a vast Moorish dynasty (see "Spain," p. 197), retained its own ambitions. Even now, extremists still consider most of the map on the previous page "Greater Morocco." (Rule of thumb: "Greater Anywhere" is bad news for the folks next door to Anywhere.) But after Berlin, France got most of Greater Morocco—*dibs!*—including Algeria, Mali, Mauritania, and more. Spain, however, got Western Sahara (in two pieces, Saguia el-Hamra and Rio de Oro). Nobody asked the Sahrawis who actually lived there.

Eventually, Morocco and Algeria each defeated the French, but in opposite fashions. Morocco's push-back involved lots of prideful Greater Morocco talk, reaching independence in 1956 without massive bloodshed. Algeria's rebellion was about socialist self-determination, but France wasn't going to give up Algeria without a horrible, protracted war. So that's what they got until 1962, killing more than 150,000 people.

Morocco assisted the Algerian rebels, since in Morocco's mind,

Algeria was part of Greater Morocco. But after the war, this was news to Algeria. Pissed off, Morocco invaded, a skirmish called the Sand War, which brought more dead bodies and a lot of glowering.

Fast-forward to 1973, when young Sahrawi rebels created the Popular Front for the Liberation of Saguia el-Hamra and Rio de Oro. (Revolutionaries truly suck at naming stuff.) Semi-acronymed as the "Polisario Front," their raids against the Spanish quickly gained popular support. By October 1975, Spain's Generalissimo Francisco Franco was approaching his famously ongoing death; given this and other more pressing concerns, Spain was ready to bail. For a time, Sahrawis seemed about to get an actual country.

However, Morocco's king, eager to be even Greater, saw a chance to grab Western Sahara's resources and stabilize his rule. Before Spain backed out, Morocco rapidly marched 300,000-plus settlers into its "Southern Provinces," cutting Spain in on the mineral rights to buy goodwill. *Finders' keepers!* To the south, Mauritania also claimed the region, so Morocco and Spain gave them the southern third in a deal brokered by Henry Kissinger, who considered Morocco an important U.S. ally. Morocco then started building a series of defensible walls, pushing the Sahrawis into the desert.

And so Sahrawi independence vanished. Piece of cake.

For its part, the UN insisted that Sahrawis had the right to self-determination, but nobody did much. Algeria gave the Sahrawis a place to crash near Tindouf, partly out of compassion, partly because Algeria was still pissed at Morocco. Polisario resumed its raids, and Mauritania soon decided the hassle wasn't worth it, letting Morocco pick up the rebound. But Polisario accomplished bupkus against the Moroccans, who eventually walled off almost every inhabitable inch. Over thirty years later, between 150,000 and 200,000 Sahrawis—the majority of the population—are *still* living in desolate tent cities named for the villages they used to call home.

Meanwhile, more than 50,000 Sahrawis remained behind in the "Southern Provinces" under Moroccan control. In the years since, independence activists have been jailed, tortured, and/or disappeared. (Morocco's willingness to shoot its own people earned the early part of this era its nickname, the "Years of Lead.") On its side, Polisario abused captured Moroccans; some remained captive until 2005.

The Organisation of African Unity (OAU) and the UN brokered a truce in 1991, with a plebescite slated for 1992. Morocco insisted (and still insists) that its settlers must be included in the vote. Sahrawis will never agree, since more Moroccans now live in Western Sahara than Sahrawis live on Earth. And that's that.

Meanwhile, Algeria has made nice with Morocco, since both are struggling with violent Islamist movements, so the Sahrawis' only real ally has no more support to give. Nonetheless, Polisario refuses to accept defeat, damning the Sahrawis to one of the harshest spots on the planet.

Still, hellish as the camps are—120-degree heat, sandstorms, no vegetation—they're at least stable enough that schools have been established. Young Sahrawis have even earned college scholarships abroad.

The place isn't without hope. It's just lacking food, water, resources, and a real future.

BONUS STRESS:
YOU GOT GHANA IN MY GUINEA

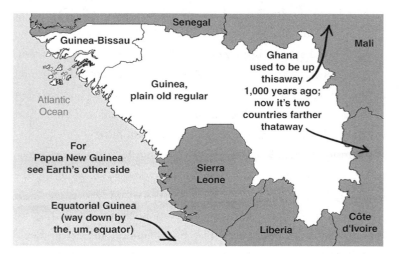

The globe currently has four Guineas—Equatorial, Bissau, regular, and Papua New—multiple Guyanas, and a Ghana, which is nowhere near Guinea, which is where Ghana was.

Confusing, yes. But we manage to keep our Yorks—England, New, Dick, and Peppermint Patty—separate. We can manage this, too.

Ghana was originally a 9th-century West African empire, right about where eastern Guinea is now, plus a chunk to the north. Modern Ghana, however, is way farther east. The UK colonized that spot, calling it Gold Coast, in 1874. In 1957, the colony became independent, and the locals took the name "Ghana" to claim a sense of lineage from the old empire, location be damned. So that's your Ghana.

Guinea happened when Portugal showed up in West Africa in the

15th century. Their colony was the first "Guinea," although it's not the one we now call by that name.

A few years later, and much farther south, Portuguese explorer Fernão do Pó also strolled into Equatorial Africa. He called the main island he found there Formosa ("beautiful"). This eventually became the name of the Asian island now called Taiwan, just to confuse you.

"Formosa," however, didn't stick. Instead, visitors soon named the African island after the explorer who found it; the Spanish version of his name was Póo. So that's what stuck for hundreds of years. And wow I had better rephrase that before we publish this.

Portugal traded Póo and some adjacent bits to Spain, so this equatorial area became *Spanish* Guinea, distinguished from *Portuguese* Guinea in West Africa.

Later on, France entered West Africa just south of Portuguese Guinea. Naturally, they called that place Guinea, too, as if they'd thought of it. Creative as hell, these colonists. But French Guinea became independent first, so that's the Guinea people call Guinea, and Portuguese Guinea next door is specified by its capital: Guinea-Bissau. Of the two, Guinea-Bissau struggles with poverty, authoritarian rule, and violence, while Guinea's government adds extra corruption as a bonus. In early 2007, a seven-week period of strikes to protest the dictator has led to shortages, nationwide instability, and more than a hundred deaths. Regular Guinea might be a bloody mess by the time you read this.

To the south, Spanish equatorial Guinea became independent as, yes, Equatorial Guinea, and the island of Póo got a new name, Bioko. That was probably worth independence right there. Modern Equatorial Guinea's government has even more brutality than it does oil. And it has loads of oil.

New Guinea is a Pacific island north of Australia, named after a complete lack of imagination. Colonial powers tried to control it for centuries, but even now, there are literally hundreds of languages and cultures still thriving in various pockets, so good luck with that. The Dutch eventually grabbed the western half, which Indonesia now claims, involving a good deal of bloodshed; the eastern half is the former English and Australian colony of Papua New Guinea, which is one of the wildest places on earth. (Nobody's completely sure where the "Papua" bit comes from.)

Guinea, incidentally, means "woman" in Susu, which is spoken where Guinea now sits. Why call it "woman"? Who knows? But it's no sillier than calling the United States of America after an explorer who never even saw the place. Although he *did* see Guyana.

Guyana (also spelled "Guiana," but that's only one letter different from "Guinea," and screw *that*) is actually the name of a geological area spanning the northeasternmost hump of South America. The word means "many rivers," which there are.

Three colonial powers each took a slice. West to east, they lined up in alphabetical order: British Guiana, Dutch Guiana, and French Guiana.

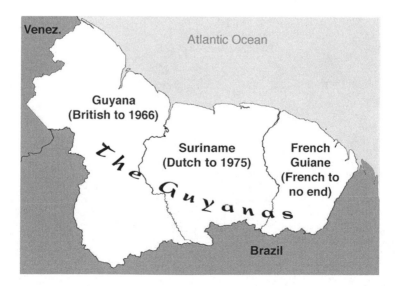

They've also become independent from left to right, as Guyana (in 1966), Suriname (in 1975), and French Guiane (never; still part of France, the way Hawaii is part of the U.S.).

Guyana (the formerly British one) is also the home country of three men accused of plotting to cause fuel explosions at JFK Airport, a plan capable of "unfathomable damage" according to the U.S. attorney and yet "virtually impossible" according to actual experts. So panic at your own discretion.

Your checklist, then, using a few of the mnemonics I used when studying for *Jeopardy!*:

Spain left Póo on the Equator. Compared with Spain, Portugal is older, smaller, and farther west; Portuguese Guinea be so ("Bissau"), too. The French came last and left first. Papua New is only half and not sure why. The Guyanas were left to right, coming and going. Ghana's not an Empire but used to be. In Guinea.

Enjoy your planet.

SOUTH ASIA

SRI LANKA

- Sinhalese government v. Tamil separatists

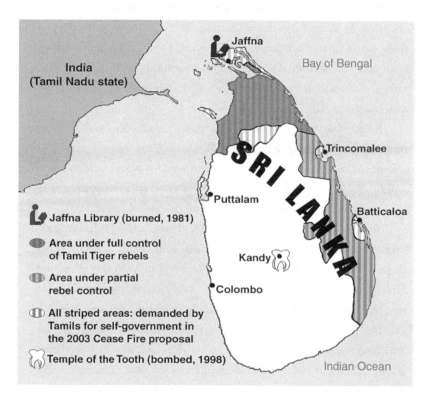

Jaffna

India (Tamil Nadu state)

Bay of Bengal

Trincomalee

Puttalam

Batticaloa

 Jaffna Library (burned, 1981)

Kandy

Colombo

Area under full control of Tamil Tiger rebels

Area under partial rebel control

All striped areas: demanded by Tamils for self-government in the 2003 Cease Fire proposal

Temple of the Tooth (bombed, 1998)

Indian Ocean

Outside its war zones, Sri Lanka has the highest standard of living in South Asia. If the two sides ever make peace, Sri Lanka could become another Singapore or Hong Kong. The Arabic name for this island, Serendib, is the root of our word for accidental beauty. Unfortunately, the rest of this entry is hideous.

About three-fourth of Sri Lankans are Buddhist Sinhalese. Most of the rest are Tamil, usually Hindu or Christian. Both groups originated in India and have shared the island for many centuries—intermixing enough that even they sometimes might have to ask who's who. Too bad they've been killing each other steadily now for decades.

In the 19th century, as West Indian plantations declined due to the abolition of slavery, the British shifted coffee and tea production to their colony here (then known as "Ceylon"), importing extra Tamils from India as indentured workers. This new influx—"Indian" Tamils, seen as distinct from the earlier "Ceylon" Tamils—got the same reception immigrant labor usually gets.

A little later, Christian missionaries set up schools on the island, teaching classes in English and Jesus. But since Christianity already had a foothold in Tamil areas, that's where most schools went. Soon some Tamils spoke fine English, receiving better employment opportunities than the majority Sinhalese. Which pissed the Sinhalese off.

So after British rule ended in 1948, the majority Sinhalese government yanked citizenship from Indian Tamils and tried to expel them back to India. The Official Language Act of 1956 also mandated Sinhala as the government tongue, excluding many Tamils from power. One-fifth of the country suddenly wasn't invited anymore.

Discrimination led to increasing calls for Tamil autonomy; the Sinhalese responded with violence, and off we go. In 1981, the Jaffna Public Library, the world's main repository of ancient, irreplaceable Tamil manuscripts—a treasure not just to Tamils but to human history itself—was burned by a Sinhalese mob.

Finally, in 1983, a separatist group called the Liberation Tigers of Tamil Eelam (the "Tamil Tigers"; *eelam* means "homeland") killed thirteen soldiers near Jaffna, beginning a civil war that has now lasted nearly a quarter-century.

In Colombo, a Sinhalese mob responded by massacring Tamils. Numerous government officials actively assisted the rioters. "Black July" shattered any hope for cooperation. More than 100,000 Tamils fled into the countryside, hid in the homes of friends, or simply left for good. Thousands joined the Tamil Tigers.

Numerous truces have failed. Both sides have broken the rules, often hideously. Both sides have killed lots of civilians, used child combatants, and tortured prisoners. But neither side has enough firepower to win, so each side just continues the grisly attrition. So far, more than 65,000 people have been killed, exceeding the U.S. death toll in Vietnam.

In the 1980s, the rebels pioneered the bomb-laden vest; "Black Tigers" have since carried out hundreds of suicide attacks ("donating yourself," they call it). So far, Tigers have "donated" themselves to killing one Sri Lankan president, wounding another, and assassinating an Indian prime minister whose peacemaking troops had committed local crimes of their own. The Tigers have also attacked Sri Lanka's Central Bank, its World Trade Center, its army headquarters in Colombo, and the international airport.

Do not piss off people who may believe in reincarnation.

The Tigers even truck-bombed the Temple of the Tooth, the Sinhalese's holiest shrine. (The Tooth is allegedly a left canine from the Buddha's own mouth.) The Colombo government quickly reassured the nation: yes, eight people had died, but the tooth was okay.

In 1994, the government tried a new strategy, called War for Peace, displaying a finely honed skill at stupidity. ("Explosions for Silence" and "Drowning for Air" might work as well.) After an all-out invasion and attacks against civilian buildings, Colombo gained Jaffna, but not peace. When your opponents wear cyanide suicide vials around their necks, mass killing is no big deterrent.

In 2002, Norwegian negotiators brokered a truce that held some promise. In theory, the Tamils would get autonomy—not necessarily independence—in the north and the east. Negotiations collapsed in 2003, but relative quiet lingered.

Then came the 2004 tsunami, which hit both sides of the island thanks to a whim of geography. Thirty thousand Sri Lankans—Sinhalese and Tamil alike—died; six thousand more were missing, presumed dead. (Proportionally, this was 9-11 multiplied by 180.) Over $1.5 billion in damage was sustained by an island where the per capita income is $4,000.

You'd think *this* might pull people together. Nope. It was mid-2005 before the two sides could agree on how to manage relief aid. By 2006, the war began flaring again, and in spring 2007, the rebels launched their first air raid, striking a government base near Colombo's main airport and causing international airlines to suspend night flights into the capital.

On and on we go, with 3,500 killed in the past year.

In August 2006, Sri Lanka's air force bombed a group of young Tamil girls, claiming they were child terrorists. The Tigers say they were learning emergency first aid in an orphanage. Neither version holds much hope for the future.

BURMA

- Dictatorship v. own citizens, anywhere
- Numerous independence movements

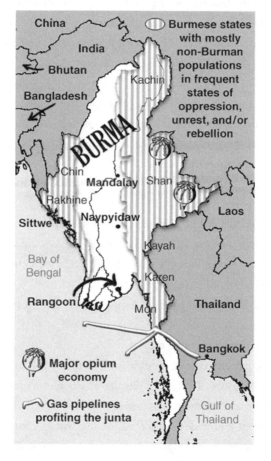

It is not power that corrupts, but fear. Fear of losing power corrupts those who wield it, and fear of the scourge of power corrupts those who are subject to it.
—Nobel Peace Prize winner Aung San Suu Kyi,
now in her 12th year of house arrest

Burma (aka Myanmar— see sidebar) is less one country than a Third World Soviet Union—a corrupt state able to control ethnically diverse lands only through police-state tactics.

While ethnic Burmans set up shop here in the 9th century, the region has never been homogenous. As Burman empires rose and fell, Mon, Shan, Kachin, Karen, Wa, and other peoples maintained their own cultures, often warring with one another, Burmans, and anyone else handy.

Still, by the 18th century, Burmans had established a dynasty bumping China in the east and British India in the west. Britain, however, didn't like being bumped; three wars later—all rationalized by the British as self-defense—Burma, which still wasn't all Burman, was annexed to British India, despite being neither British nor Indian.

This was going to work out brilliantly.

Most of Burma didn't colonize easily, despite Britain's willingness to flatten entire villages. In 1937, however, the UK finally deemed Burma as separate from India, which was like declaring France not part of Spain. By 1941, some young Burmese radicals (the "Thirty Comrades") scooted off to the Japanese Empire. To begin training as anti-imperialist fighters.

That went just brilliantly, too.

Sure enough, the British were driven off, only to be supplanted by the Japanese. Whoops. To their credit, the Thirty Comrades eventually changed tactics and resisted the Japanese. One empire down, one to go.

The Thirty Comrades' leader was Aung San, a charismatic nationalist. While in Japan's puppet Burmese government, Aung San secretly contacted the British in India and soon went all *Hogan's Heroes* on the Japanese. After the war, Aung San also led the drive for Burmese independence before being assassinated by rivals, turning him into the martyred father of Burmese nationhood. He was survived by a daughter, Aung San Suu Kyi, who will reappear in four paragraphs.

Independence came in 1948, but with little planning for ethnic and regional issues; Karen, Rakhine, and Mon people were largely excluded. Burma's potential dissolution was also baked in, with possible independence for the Kachin, Kayah, and Shan on the table from the get-go.

Karen people rebelled immediately; they had sided against Burmans during both the British and Japanese occupations, so they got a faceful of Burman war crimes in response, a situation that still flares periodically. And while several communist factions competed for power in Rangoon, in the countryside some non-Burman ethnic groups often pursued their own interests as if Burma didn't even exist. Some generated serious income from narcotics.

In 1962, a military coup tried to end such factionalism, in some measure simply by shooting the factions. Hundreds of people were arrested and/or killed, and soon all opposition parties were banned. Armed rebellions surged in Kachin and Shan areas, and the cycle of revolt and crackdown increased.

A few bad decades later, economic woes led to a widespread uprising on August 8, 1988. This "8888" revolt led to an even *more* brutal dictatorship, plus the rise of Aung San's daughter, Aung San Suu Kyi, as a leader of nonviolent democratic resistance.

The newest junta, the State Law and Order Restoration Council (SLORC), staged surprisingly free elections in 1990; however, when Suu Kyi's party won a landslide, the SLORC arrested the leaders and refused to relinquish power. The human rights situation went from terrible to tragic, with thousands of people seized as political prisoners, children pressed into military service, and widespread forced labor.

While the situation has its ebb and flow—Suu Kyi is released from house arrest, then rearrested; peace is made with a rebel group, then fighting restarts—that's where things still stand. The SLORC is

"BURMA" V. "MYANMAR"

In Burmese, *m* is often shortened into *b*, and *r* can become *y*. (If that sounds inconsistent, say the sentence "Tough ploughs fought through troughs, dough, and hiccoughs," and reconsider.) So *Myanma* and *Burma* are the same words, as are *Rangoon* and *Yangon*, just spoken with different markers of social class.

In 1989, SLORC declared that the English name should be *Myanmar*, with an *r*. (In British English, that final *r* just lengthens the sound, sheeplike: *Myanmaaaaa*. Which is what SLORC was aiming for.) The UN went along, but the democracy movement insisted on *Burma*. U.S. and UK politicians then stuck with *Burma*, too. I've tried to maintain UN usages, but here I'd rather line up with the Nobel Peace Prize winner than the murderous junta. This is an empty gesture, of course; what matters is people not getting killed, and most Burmese would probably be cool with calling it *Banana* if everybody got to vote, eat, work, and speak without fear.

now the State Peace and Development Council (SPDC), but it's the same deal.

Despite lacking any credible threat to its borders, Burma spends roughly half of its budget on its army, now the largest in Southeast Asia. Bizarrely, the junta has also recently moved its capital from Rangoon to the inland town of Naypyidaw, a nine-hour train ride from the nation's biggest city, port, and center of trade. It's unclear why.

More central to the various conflicts? Farther from an imagined landing of U.S. Marines? Closer to the opium fields? The advice of an as-
trologer? In any case: more land confiscated, more forced labor, and
more waste of resources.

Strangely, Burma's mixture of the exotic, forbidden, and incomprehensible has lately turned it into an exciting tourist destination for
many Europeans and Asians. However, much of the hospitality infrastructure was built with forced labor on confiscated lands, with profits
going to the regime and its cronies. So while the Burmese are happy to
see you, and some of your money may help a few directly, your visit
helps sustain their oppression. Suu Kyi and her supporters implore you
not to visit.

You are also usually discouraged from buying teak, which benefits
the junta, and you are asked to protest against Chevron, Total, Schlum-
berger, and other Western companies whose gas pipelines provide billions in income to the regime.

Unfortunately, those aren't the only companies doing business
here. China's oil companies are involved in a big way. India is hot to
build a new pipeline near Sittwe. Malaysia's national oil company just
showed up with flowers. Corporations from Japan, Singapore, Thailand, Russia, and South Korea have all planted flags. Even North
Korea has recently dropped by for a chat.

So I'm not buying teak, and I'm not hobnobbing in Rangoon.
Unfortunately for the people of Burma, I'm also not buying a giant
Chinese corporation.

KASHMIR

- Pakistan v. India
- China v. India (dormant)
- Kashmir separatists v. everybody (but India mostly)

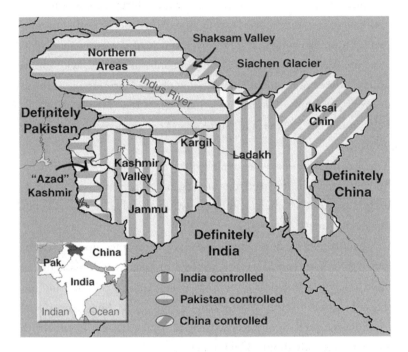

That India is on Siachen [glacier], and in control of it,
is a sign that we can be a superpower.
—INDIAN LT. COL. J. S. PUNDIR TO *TIME* MAGAZINE,
BOASTING OVER AN UNINHABITABLE WASTELAND

India is massive and diverse, with one-sixth of the planet's population and twenty-three official languages. Naturally, India has struggled with separatists since independence, from 1950s Tamil nationalists to secessionist movements dotting India's northeast, where Assamese nationalists are currently arguing not just with India over autonomy but with one another over whether the spelling is *Assam* or *Asom*.

Of all the subcontinent's hot spots, Kashmir is the most persistent. With the world's first-, second-, and sixth-biggest countries all pushing into one another, this seems almost inevitable.

When India and Pakistan gained independence in 1947, the 565 autonomous "princely states" under British rule had to pick a team. However, while the state of Jammu and Kashmir was mostly Muslim, its maharaja was a Hindu who thought he could remain independent by playing the big boys against each other. Two months later, Pashtuns from North Waziristan (see "Afghanistan/Pakistan," p. 11) tried to settle the matter by barging in with Pakistani government support. The maharaja asked for India's help, and up came the troops. (It's also possible India cruised in before they'd been invited.) Welcome to the First Kashmir War.

About sixteen months and five thousand dead soldiers later, a UN-negotiated truce created an acknowledged Line of Control between Indian and Pakistani forces. This is still essentially the boundary to this day. Pakistan got Azad ("liberated") Kashmir and the Northern Areas, including the Shaksam Valley. India got the Kashmir Valley, Jammu, and Ladakh, including Aksai Chin.

Nobody got the Siachen Glacier, because it's a strategically useless, uninhabitable mountain area high enough to induce altitude sickness and even convulsions. No one could possibly be insane enough to fight over it.

We'll get back to Siachen soon. You sense what's coming.

The truce specified that the people of Kashmir would simply vote on which country to join. Never happened. Both India and Pakistan still basically claim all of Kashmir.

To the east, after the communist revolution, China began stomping into Tibet, which itself has historically claimed chunks of Kashmir. In consolidating the occupation, China grabbed Aksai Chin from India in 1962. India still claims Aksai Chin, but it's a virtually uninhabited salt plain, and India seems to have decided it's not worth the hassle. The de facto border has been stable for decades.

Pakistan transferred the Shaksam Valley to China in 1963, buying goodwill from the bigger kid before the Second Kashmir War against India began in 1965. Two months and eight thousand more dead soldiers later, the UN imposed yet another cease-fire, returning everybody back to their starting positions.

Nobody thought Siachen counted for squat yet. Soon, though.

India and Pakistan next fought in 1971 over a different postcolonial mess: independence for East Pakistan (now Bangladesh). After nine months of carnage in Bangladesh and two weeks of fighting directly between India and Pakistan, the latter finally conceded. The armistice essentially formalized the Line of Control in Kashmir, promising "lasting peace." We've heard that one before.

Siachen still didn't get even a simple dotted line down the middle. Only mountain climbers even cared. But U.S. maps put Siachen in Pakistan's territory, so climbers tended to ask Pakistan for permission to dangle. Pakistan soon thought of Siachen as theirs.

However, in the late 1970s, an Indian expedition took a hike around Siachen. Pakistan's soldiers noticed. The freak-out began. Both countries suddenly considered a glacier three miles in the air as a valid military objective. In 1984, Pakistan decided to sneak in some permanent troops, but India found out when Pakistan ordered cold-weather gear from the same British store where India bought stuff. (Really.) This may have been the first war in which a key military supplier also sold fuzzy earmuffs. The race was on. India got to the top first, winning the right to . . . stand on an empty glacier. *Victory is mine!*

Pakistan arrived a few days later, and people started shooting.

However, most of the casualties haven't been from bullets, but from frostbite, oxygen deprivation, and avalanches.

In 1987, Pervez Musharraf led some Pakistani commandos onto the glacier. This effort was repelled, but in 1999, Musharraf—by now a general—sent soldiers onto a 15,000-foot-high ridge at Kargil, hoping to cut supply to India's highest outposts. India quickly rebuffed this effort, too, but the Kargil War endangered hundreds of millions of lives; both sides had tested nuclear weapons the previous year. Fortunately, the nukes stayed holstered, but Pakistan's loss helped destabilize its government sufficiently for Musharraf to seize power. He has remained Pakistan's supremo ever since, not to mention the guy the U.S. War on Terror largely hinges on.

Siachen's toll so far: perhaps three to five thousand men. Economic cost: half a billion dollars per year, from countries with tens of millions of malnourished children. Just to remind you: people are fighting 3,000 feet *above* the altitude many paragliders avoid in order to prevent hallucinations. But despite a 2003 truce, each side keeps a few thousand men in place, just in case. Peace might be easier if the president of one side hadn't personally launched two sneak attacks.

Meanwhile, an additional factor has recently emerged: local militants, some pro–Pakistan, some pro-independence. Most are centered in the Muslim-majority, densely populated Kashmir Valley, but attacks reach into India itself. Besides several train bombings, in December 2001, the Indian parliament was suicide-attacked by five gunmen. India blamed the raid on Lashkar-e-Toiba ("Soldiers of the Pure"), backed by Pakistan, leading to renewed nuclear tension in 2002.

Fortunately, India/Pakistan relations have thawed considerably. Violence discourages international investment, so both countries have economic as well as moral reasons for peace in Kashmir. However, there's no obvious solution.

Neither India nor Pakistan will get the whole pie, of course.

Independence for Kashmir, itself split between Hindus and Muslims, would probably just create another civil war, so that's not an option either.

India would gladly accept the Line of Control as the permanent boundary, and that's what the West leans toward as a lasting solution. But this gives India the Kashmir Valley, which is 95 percent Muslim. Neither Pakistan nor Kashmiri nationalists would say yes.

Granting independence only to the Kashmir Valley would solve several problems, but it would also create two more: (a) both Pakistan and India would have to surrender territory, which isn't likely, and (b) it would validate other separatists all over both countries, possibly destabilizing the entire region.

Meanwhile, given the fanatics on both sides, neither government can be seen as giving too much; after all, that's how even Gandhi got killed.

NEPAL (WITH BHUTAN ADDED FOR EXTRA ENLIGHTENMENT)

I n the Himalayas lie two ancient lands, one Hindu, one Buddhist, both undergoing enormous change.

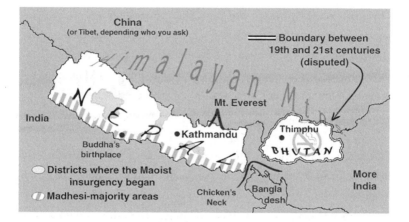

NEPAL

- Maoist rebellion v. royalty; tentative peace, 2006
- Possible Madhesi insurgency, early 2007

While Nepal is associated with the vast Himalayas, it's not all backpackers and chai tea. Kathmandu has Detroit's population, packed eight times more densely and with twice the air pollution.

Until recently, Nepal was ruled by the Shah family (no relation to Iran), who united the country via conquest 250 years ago. However, in the 19th century a rival clan called the Ranas took over, running Nepal through family connections sort of the way Tony Soprano ran New Jersey. The Ranas and Shahs have played *Family Feud* ever since.

The Ranas saw isolation as a way to retain power, but they also kowtowed to the British rulers of India, so rich Nepalese often got liberal educations at Oxford and Eton. After WWII, India gained independence and built the world's largest democracy, so by the 1950s, anti-Rana, pro-democracy sentiment grew among the upper class.

India decided that installing the rival Shah family atop a democracy would turn Nepal into a stable bulwark between them and China. Once in charge, however, the new Shah king abolished parliament, seizing power. In 1991, popular pressure led to a constitutional monarchy, but the king's power was only somewhat reduced. When life for most people didn't improve, strikes and riots followed. The king responded with violence, so a Maoist insurgency declared their own local governments in rural areas and began a protracted civil war.

By 2001, the Shah heir apparent was Dipendra Bir Bikram Shah Dev, age twenty-nine, an Eton grad with a taste for booze who had been nicknamed "Dippy" by his classmates. Unfortunately, Dippy fell madly for a hot twenty-two-year-old named Devyani Rana.

Notice her last name. Romeo and Juliet had nothing on these two.

The Shah family disapproved of the union, so Dippy disapproved of his family. With an M-16 rifle. On June 1, 2001, Dippy went *Scarface* on nearly the entire royal house, killing nine, before turning a gun on himself. (For her part, Dippy's ex now lives in India and seems a fine young lady, if not quite worth machine-gunning your family over.) The Maoist insurgency saw this as a chance to redouble their pressure, and the new king, Dippy's uncle Gyanendra (a family Shemp who wasn't around when things went postal), was unable to handle the challenge.

Peace talks failed, and as the Maoists took the countryside, Gyanendra cracked down on opposition politicians and the press. Hundreds of journalists were jailed; many were tortured. Nepalese newspapers took to printing blank editorial pages in protest.

Thirteen thousand people died in the civil war, with human rights violations committed by both sides. The violence depressed the much-needed tourist trade, amplifying everyone's desperation. Finally, in late 2005, an alliance of seven political parties and the Maoist rebellion signed an accord for a new try at democracy. To convince the king to go along, the agreement called for mass protests. Despite Gyanendra's last-ditch gunfire and tear gas, the demonstrations continued for three solid weeks.

Ultimately, Gyanendra gave in. The new parliament stripped the king of his authority, not to mention his status as a descendant of Vishnu. And as of early 2007, the Maoist leaders have locked up their weapons (the UN holds the keys) and joined in a new government, serving as a temporary cabinet to the prime minister. Things may work.

Or not. At this writing, lowland Madhesi people, who make up perhaps a third of Nepal's population and have rarely had much say, have begun mostly nonviolent protests for fuller representation. So far, federal police have responded harshly, some Madhesis have escalated, and dozens are dead. By the time you read this, either the Madhesis will have more representation, or another insurgency may have begun.

BHUTAN

Until 1964, Bhutan could be reached only by hiking in from Tibet. Radio didn't exist until 1973, the first airport wasn't built until 1983, and Bhutan didn't get Internet access until 2000. At least they missed CompuServe.

To this day, tourism is tightly controlled, limiting the number of Westerners allowed to Coke up the place. What visitors find is often enchanting—shot-put tournaments, butter tea, and lovely traditional garments. However, wearing that traditional dress is mandatory, not a choice, and that tells you a lot. Some Bhutanese are chafing to wear blue jeans, eat french fries, and interact with the outside world.

Satellite TV now features broadcasts from India and the West. (There's also the official Bhutan Broadcasting Service, which the Bhutanese watch as much as you do.) It's hard to imagine the shock caused by the first glimpse of, say, pro wrestling; after lifetimes of seeking placid moderation, the sight of 300-pound musclemen slapping each other for no reason must have been mind-blowing. Pretty soon, the government yanked the show off the air, but schoolkids in monkish garb still practice *Wrestlemania* moves.

Bhutan's king Jigme Singye Wangchuck long attempted to balance modernization with respect for tradition. Wangchuck recently made the entire country a nonsmoking area—the only such nation on Earth—and is notable for saying that "Gross National Happiness" is more important than Gross National Product. Then again, the king has ten children by four queens, all of whom are sisters. *Dear Penthouse: I never thought this would happen to me.* So *he's* probably pretty happy, at least.

The only military conflict here is the occasional need to expel Assamese separatists camping near the Chicken's Neck back into India. That said, China is reportedly building roads on Bhutan's undefended northern border, perhaps planning a land grab. Bhutan could get Tibetted.

At this writing, King Wangchuck has suddenly resigned. It's not clear yet why; perhaps he's just tired of tourists asking him to sing "Everybody Have Fun Tonight." His eldest son will now rule in his stead, and 2008 elections may lead to the country's first parliament, which will surely struggle with globalization, China, and most of all the fascinating conflict between an isolated 19th-century nation and a 21st-century world.

The 21st century seems to be gaining strength.

EAST AND SOUTHEAST ASIA

NORTH KOREA*

- Kim Jong-Il's regime v. South Korea, the U.S., and North Koreans

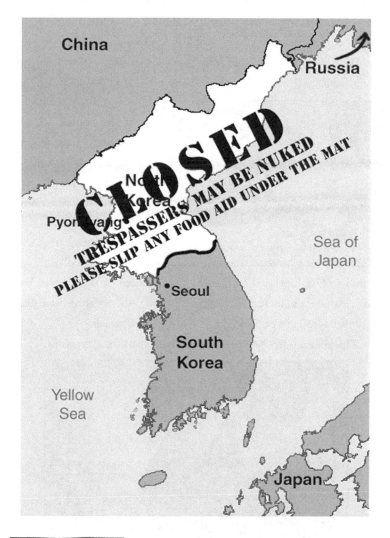

———————

*The official name is the Democratic People's Republic of Korea. However, the first three words are lies. I have a limit of two lies per country name.

Some dictatorships have presidents-for-life; Kim Il-Sung has been "Eternal President" for thirteen years. Despite being dead. The anthem to his memory opens with blood-soaked hillsides. *Ewww.* And North Korea's calendar places the beginning of time at Kim Il-Sung's birth. It's not 2007 in Pyongyang; it's 96.

Weird enough for you? Now here's an official North Korean poster from 2003:

Yikes. That's a U.S. soldier being smashed by the mighty force of . . . um . . . unarmed North Korean hands. With beautiful nails.

Notice that's a *U.S.* missile, not one of theirs. The caption: "With the united power of the nation, let's smash America's nuclear war provocations!" Ah. So there's surprisingly little pretense of having any real means to attack.

This one shouts "Merciless punishment for U.S. imperialists!":

Run! That North Korean is single-handedly destroying the Capitol with . . . um . . . three giant bullets. Carried in by hand. These posters are clearly designed to inspire people who have exactly squat. Which they do. Let's back up and see how they got that way.

KIM IL-SUNG

The current dictator's dad fought the Japanese occupation in the 1930s, joining Chinese communists and then the Soviet army. After WWII, Kim began liquidating his rivals, and in 1948, the Soviets made Kim prime minister.

In 1950, Kim ordered his army to invade the South. They soon took almost the entire peninsula, but the U.S. and the UN pushed back almost to the Chinese border—far enough that the Chinese themselves pushed back. Finally, in 1953, everybody agreed on a boundary at roughly the 38th parallel. Right where it had been, pretty much. So three million people died for essentially no result.

Lacking an actual peace treaty, the two sides are still technically at war. You've seen Quentin Tarantino films: in a standoff, nobody wants to be the first to lower his gun. So for half a century, the U.S. turned South Korea into a forward military base, while the Soviets and China took turns arming the North.

Incidentally, the South wasn't terribly free right away, with decades of rigged elections and corruption. Real democracy took thirty years. But in the North, Kim used his position mostly to kill more North Koreans, consolidating power permanently. Forced labor and subservience became the rule, and Kim needed only to point across the 38th parallel to claim everything he did was self-defense. This was horseshit, but plausible horseshit. Many North Koreans bought in.

Kim also seems to have gone quite mad, with deadly results. Claims of magic powers and his mandatory "Great Leader" nickname are amusing, but Kim's mandatory *Juche*—total self-reliance for a densely populated country with limited resources—has led to health care shortages, rural non-development, and famine. Juche is idiotic. And it's official state policy.

After the Soviet collapse, North Korea became extremely isolated, but that fed right into Juche, so the airlock sealed both ways. Juche is now the required purpose of all North Korean art, music, and mass communications. Millions inside North Korea may have little idea that any other sort of lifestyle exists. Underground journalism? A secret rebel movement? No such thing, apparently. George Orwell would plotz.

When Kim Il-Sung died, grief was enforced under penalty of law.

KIM JONG-IL

Dear Leader is an irresistibly comic villain: five-foot-two, with a pompadour and four-inch lifts in his shoes. He dresses like Dr. Evil, loves James Bond movies, and once kidnapped a prominent South Korean actress and her film-director husband, hoping to improve the North Korean movie industry. The result: a monster movie in which a lizard-shaped rice ball turns into a monster that eats iron. He brings peace to the village but then eats the heroine and dies. I have *got* to put that in the Netflix queue.

However, according to defectors, Kim Jong-Il is harsher than his dad was, more willing to starve and torture his own people, and more obsessed with his own cult.

And that's almost all we know.

Boy Kim has spoken in public exactly once, shouting: "Glory to the heroic soldiers of the People's Army!" And that does seem to be his only priority: Kim's army gets first dibs on funding, housing, medicine, clothing, and food. All told, North Korea spends more of its GNP on its army than does any other country on earth.

Scary, but per capita income is three bucks a day. The roads are

empty. People starve. It's a *prison*. So a high percentage of GNP, by itself, spent on weapons doesn't inevitably make the country a threat to
others. Many of the guns are pointed inward.

Most of the country is stunningly poor. Without international aid,
millions would starve—and after the Soviet collapse, that's exactly
what happened. Between 2 and 3 million North Koreans died of
hunger in the 1990s. The entire population is roughly 23 million. So,
sure, 20 percent of the male population of military age is in the army,
but *the army gets fed first*. Of course people join.

So yes, Dear Leader is a violent, sociopathic freak. Yup. But if it
were up to me, I'd carpet-bomb the country with food for a year, with
every item marked "Gift of the U.S. and South Korea." The rest might
take care of itself.

The main apparent obstacle: North Korea's nuclear program.

THE NUKES

In 2006, North Korea detonated its first nuclear device. But the blast
was perhaps as little as 1 percent of the bomb the United States
dropped on Nagasaki about sixty years ago. And North Korea had no-
tified the Chinese to expect a shake over ten times bigger. So, fizzle.

That was North Korea's one nuclear test. Ever. And it used up over
10 percent of the country's plutonium. It's not nothing, but it's comparatively flea-sized. Any attempt to use one of these half-assed weapons
would be instant suicide. And even if Kim Jong-Il *were* suicidal, the nukes
would have to be squeezed into missile-friendly size and weight. There's
no evidence of North Korea managing any such thing. And even given
that, they'd need missiles. North Korea's best long-range missile is the No
Dong model (I'm leaving that name alone), a modified Scud familiar
from the 1991 Iraq/Kuwait war. They've got a few others that could
threaten their neighbors, and that's no small thing. But thoughts of a
North Korean attack on the United States are utter paranoia.

So why build these weapons, then? North Korea's conventional self-defenses are rusting apart. Plus, they're broke beyond belief, and missile sales to other pariah states are one of the few sources of income they have left.

And why the anti-U.S. posters? Dictatorships need enemies. Otherwise, starving North Koreans would have only Kim Jong-Il to blame. He's a lunatic, but he's not stupid.

THE FUTURE

In the past, Kim Jong-Il has been willing to trade nuclear stoppages for aid, and in early 2007, that's precisely the deal on the table, although it wasn't widely reported in the Western broadcast media for over twenty-four hours because North Korea changed its stance on the same day Anna Nicole Smith died. (Seriously.)

In any case, the U.S. may not need to do anything. The Koreans themselves are on it.

A generation of Koreans has reached midlife with no memory of the Korean War; their kids don't even remember the Cold War. With families split across the border, both sides realize that war would be ruinous, and—perhaps most important—conglomerates like Samsung and Hyundai would like to market to the one-third of the country north of the border.

Unification is already happening—gradually. North and South have competed as one "Korea" in several international events, TV ads in the South now feature stars from both countries, and the 2008 unified Korean Olympic team plans to travel together to Beijing on a rail line through North Korea, an unprecedented opening. Baby steps. Patience.

(Reunification will be an unholy mess, incidentally. Germany is still trying to pull things together fifteen years later—see "Germany," p. 202—and North Korea is vastly poorer than East Germany was, with a higher ratio of people to integrate. Plus, after long isolation, North Koreans will be seriously freaky. East Berlin didn't have a different *calendar.*)

Bottom line: the son groomed by Kim Jong-Il as his replacement fell out of favor in 2001 . . . for sneaking off to Disneyland.

Juche, my ass.

THAILAND

- Bangkok v. Pattani separatists
- Military coup in Bangkok, claiming to save democracy from its elected leader

ineteenth-century kings of Siam had more to worry about than getting Deborah Kerr to teach their kids English by singing Rodgers and Hammerstein.* They were also surrounded by European powers.

Great Britain controlled Burma to the west, while to the east, the French had colonized what are now called (at the price of a few million lives) Vietnam, Cambodia, and Laos. Siamese kings spent considerable energy positioning themselves as an independent buffer between two great powers.

But Britain also controlled the Malay peninsula to the south, which at the time was a series of Muslim sultanates. In negotiating with Siam over *that* boundary, the British caved on the Pattani region to buy Siamese goodwill against the French. (Nobody asked anyone in Pattani for their input.) The Muslim south has been isolated between two worlds ever since.

Siam became *Thailand,* a name carrying a nationalist streak, in 1939 while cheering for the wrong side in WWII. In the Vietnam War period, the U.S. saw Thailand as an anticommunist buffer zone, so the U.S. propped up Thai military governments until 1975, when Vietnam tragically fell into the hands of the Vietnamese. Pattani separatism was generally squished in this period.

Thailand's current king, Bhumibol Adulyadej, is much beloved, and not just because disrespecting him is considered both offensive and illegal. For one, the guy's a jazz musician who puts his mp3s online. You don't always expect that in your king of Thailand. More important, Bhumibol has usually leaned toward democracy.

However, in 2006, Bhumibol sided with a military coup claiming

---

*Incidentally, *The King and I* is banned in Thailand as false and insulting to the royal family. Even discussing the subject is frowned upon. While visiting, whenever you feel afraid, do *not* whistle a happy tune.

The King looms near the Democracy Monument.

to save Thai democracy from its own prime minister, a Ted Turner–ish billionaire named Thaksin Shinawatra. In the late 1990s, Thaksin and his allies had formed the Thai Rak Thai ("Thais Love Thais") party, an amalgamation of populist factions. Thaksin spent heavily on his campaigns, winning the prime ministership in 2001. However, as Thaksin's power increased, charges of nepotism and corruption did, too. Thaksin's 2006 sale of his broadcast company to a Singapore firm, on which he made almost $2 billion without paying a dime of tax, was seen by many as a betrayal of the nation.

Thaksin was also widely criticized for his handling of Pattani, where violence escalated steeply during his tenure. Somebody in Pattani now gets shot, blown up, or beheaded about twice a week. Bombings are often well coordinated, with multiple devices exploding simultaneously. So far, around 1,500 people—including many bystanders—have been killed in the insurgency. Thaksin eventually declared martial law in Thailand's southernmost provinces, where police already enjoyed near-impunity. Hundreds of suspects have died in custody. But the rebel attacks continue.

In 2006, in advance of Thaksin's possible reelection, the Thai army overthrew his government, reportedly with the king's consent. Next came the typical post-coup laundry list: media censorship, martial law, and severe restrictions on getting to know you. (Getting to know all about you was banned completely.)

However, the junta insists they have every intention of restoring democracy just as soon as they figure out how. So far, they've issued guidelines for a new constitution, several of which may prevent another Thaksin, and elections are tentatively scheduled for late 2007. So far so good, maybe.

In the south, however, the bombings and murders continued just days after the coup, and the military responded with even greater violence. A few weeks later, New Year celebrations brought a series of unsolved bombings to Bangkok. The military claims these were the work of some unspecified pro-Thaksin faction. The coordination of the bombings, however, points to Pattani. The insurgency may now be reaching the capital. In any case, there's no lid on violence in the Pattani region itself, and worrisome evidence of ongoing connections between the insurgents and the Islamist Jamaah Islamiyah (see "Indonesia," p. 132).

As a side issue, the Strait of Malacca is a vital shipping lane, but difficult enough to navigate that large vessels must move slowly through a poor area with weak law enforcement. The result? Pirates. Surprisingly few look like Johnny Depp. The pirates are not on anyone's side in the above conflicts. Because they're *pirates. Ahrrr.*

In any case, both the Thaksin faction and the military government have recently hired powerful U.S. public relations firms. The meaning of the word *democracy* may simply be defined by the highest bidder. So at least some of the Western system is definitely catching on.

LAOS

- Laotian army v. Hmong-in-hiding

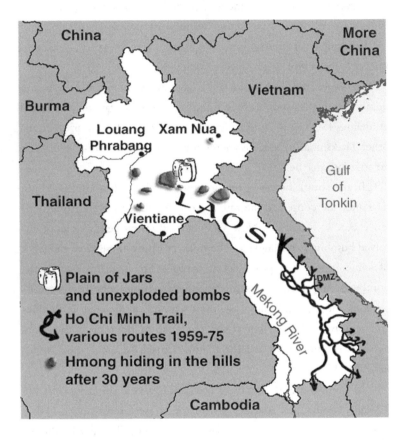

China

More
China

Vietnam

Burma

Louang Xam Nua
Phrabang

Gulf
of
Tonkin

Thailand

Vientiane

LAOS

Plain of Jars
and unexploded bombs

Ho Chi Minh Trail,
various routes 1959-75

Hmong hiding in the hills
after 30 years

Mekong River

DMZ

Cambodia

L aos descends from the medieval kingdom of Lan Xang,
"Million Elephants," the most brilliant country name ever. If I
were armed only with 14th-century technology, no way I'd
invade a place called "Million Elephants." Because, well, elephants.

Under French colonial rule, Laos had a capital at Vientiane and a
royal residence at Louang Phrabang. However, after WWII, a commu-

nist movement called the Pathet Lao ("Land of the Lao") grew as French authority declined. The Pathet Lao soon took much of the north, declaring their own capital at Xam Nua.

Next door in Vietnam, the French were defeated by Ho Chi Minh's communists in 1954. France bailed, but the U.S. saw Vietnam as a major domino in their theory of communist expansion, so the U.S. became invested in keeping a pro-Western government in South Vietnam at almost any cost.

Laos was neutral regarding Vietnam, thanks to a 1962 agreement signed in Geneva. However, the lack of French support left the Vientiane government weak, and the communist Pathet Lao grew. Meanwhile, North Vietnamese communists were using Laos to supply their allies in South Vietnam, bypassing the "peacekeeping" demilitarized zone (DMZ) via a series of ancient Laotian trading routes. (This became known in the United States as the Ho Chi Minh Trail, but in Vietnam, it was called the Truong Son Strategic Supply Route. Once again, insurgents totally suck at naming stuff.) The Pathet Lao became key allies in keeping this wagon train running.

The U.S. might simply have sent its own troops to destroy the Ho Chi Minh Trail™, but the Geneva agreement legally forbade this. So the U.S. began one of its largest covert operations ever, now simply known as The Secret War.

The CIA recruited a secret army of local Hmong people, whose language and rural culture are as different from Lao as Apache is from Mexican. Hmong are traditionally looked down upon by many Lao as primitive hicks, so the U.S. merely had to promise the Hmong a chance to fight the Lao and maybe win some autonomy, and soon the Hmong were engaging both the Pathet Lao and the North Vietnamese army.

In 1964, the U.S. also began massive bombing campaigns against the Trail™ and communist-held countryside. Laos soon became one of the most densely bombed pieces of land in history, although the loud explosions were kept quiet in the U.S. media. Much action centered around the Plain of Jars, a giant mysterious field of, yes, *jars*—thousands of huge ancient earthen containers, a Stonehenge-meets-Tupperware. This water supply/mortuary/pantry nonetheless became a Pathet Lao stronghold.

The Ho Chi Minh Trail was never shut down. By the time the United States withdrew, the Trail™ was well maintained enough to drive large vehicles the entire length, despite Hmong sacrifices comparable to all U.S. losses from the war.

Once the U.S. withdrew and the Pathet Lao seized Vientiane, the Hmong were suddenly on their own, with no supplies and no foreign allies. This was a bad time to speak a language with sixty-eight distinct sounds.* While Hmong not associated with the fighting survived the communist takeover as second-class citizens, hundreds of thousands were forced to flee. Many resettled in Thailand or the United States. Tens of thousands of others, however, saw no way out, grabbed their families, and fled into the mountainous jungle.

Thirty years later, perhaps ten thousand or more . . . are still there.

The Lao government seems to consider the whole group as an active insurgency, but by now, the Hmong-in-hiding reportedly consist of barely armed, elderly fighters, plus their wives, children, and even grandchildren whose greatest sin was to be born unwisely. These unfortunates have apparently never known life beyond clawing through jungle, eating roots, and staying one step ahead of the Laotian army. Refugees in Thailand describe being tracked and

---

*The Hmong language is also pronounced in up to twelve different tones, including "breathy" and "creaky." As a result, *Hmong* is also transliterated as *Mong, Hmao, Meo, Miao, Hmoob,* and so on. There's clearly an *m* and an *o* involved, but beyond that, you're *s* out of *l*.

hunted almost like wild game; they further claim that virtually all Hmong-in-hiding would surrender if the UN would ensure fair treatment. So far, the UN and the rest of the world haven't bothered. So thousands of exhausted Hmong-in-hiding have surrendered piecemeal over the years, taking their chances with the Laotian army. What happens to them next is fuzzy; reported fates range from resettlement and assistance to hostile indifference to execution. We'd know more, but the Laotian government denies any problem exists while keeping the area completely off-limits.

Meanwhile, Hmong resentment of Lao rule in the rest of the country continues to surface, which hasn't helped. Since 2004, after a few small attacks by something called the Lao Citizens Movement for Democracy, the Laotian government seems to have escalated its effort to delete the Hmong-in-hiding for good. By the time you read this, some of the floating blobs on the map—representing the last remaining mountain hiding spots—may be about as real as a million elephants.

P.S. If you ever visit, it's illegal for a foreigner to have a one-night stand with a Laotian. It's also illegal to preach religion of any kind. Generally, avoid the words "Oh, god, oh, god," and you should be fine.

INDONESIA

- Aceh: Muslim Separatists v. Jakarta
- Bali: Muslims v. Hindus and Westerners
- Kalimantan: Dayaks v. Madurese
- Moluccas and Sulawesi: Christians v. Muslims
- Jakarta, Bali, and throughout: Jemaah Islamiyah v. Jakarta and the West
- Papua: Jakarta v. Papuan population

omprised of six thousand populated islands scattered across an area the size of the continental United States, Indonesia is less a country than a collage, with more than 240 million people from hundreds of distinct ethnicities speaking more than three hundred local languages.

What unifies this mix? Islam, which also divides the country; the Indonesian language, although most people use other languages in daily life; and a shared history of getting one's butt kicked by Dutch colonists and Indonesian governments.

Not much to build anthems around, despite Jakarta's efforts.

Oh—and the country sits on the edge of three tectonic plates, and its southern rim is lined with volcanoes. Plus, thousands of miles of narrow shipping lanes make for a pirate wonderland. But besides that, life is good.

About half of the country's population—over 120 million people—are crammed onto the island of Java. We're talking dense: imagine the entire U.S. population west of the Mississippi River crammed into an area smaller than Arkansas. Java dominates Indonesian politics; its biggest city, Jakarta, is the capital, and every president and/or dictator but one since independence has come from the island.

Naturally, this creates tensions in the hinterlands. There's not room here to describe them all in depth; for an example that might help contextualize the rest, see "East Timor," p. 139.

ACEH

The tip of Sumatra was Islam's first beachhead in Southeast Asia; the religion has been a profound part of Acehnese life for a thousand years. Aceh was a powerful state as late as the 19th century, and it took Dutch colonists over fifteen years to control the place, accomplished by eliminating entire villages, numerous religious leaders, and thousands of people. The Acehnese are still a little twitchy about being bossed around.

After WWII and Indonesia's war of independence, Jakarta lumped Aceh together with the not-so-Islamic rest of northern Sumatra. When Aceh took up arms—escalating in the 1970s as oil companies moved in—Jakarta responded the way dictatorships do. A bloody mess ensued, lasting until Boxing Day of 2004, when a massive tsunami killed more than 120,000 people—almost 3 percent of Aceh's entire population—and left another 10 percent homeless.

The good news: unlike Sri Lanka, the tsunami led to a peace treaty between the Acehnese rebels and Jakarta. The bad news: lots of

Acehnese see the tsunami as divine punishment for being insufficiently
Islamic. So, while Aceh now has greater autonomy, it also has Sharia
law. Freedom: win some, lose some.

BALI

In 1906, the Balinese royal family found surrender to colonial rule so
humiliating that they committed public mass suicide. Today, the island
is a popular tourist destination, the very beach where the Dutch first
landed is flanked by Pizza Huts and KFCs, and many Balinese supple-
ment their incomes by dancing and reenacting their history for First
World tourists.

Mass suicide. Two shows daily.

Bali is Indonesia's only Hindu-majority island, its culture places a
singular emphasis on the arts, and the waves here make for world-class
surfing. As a result, Bali has been Indonesia's most popular tourist destination for decades, becoming much wealthier than neighboring is-

lands. Some "Balinese" crafts are even farmed out to poorer Javans, who can feel like Mexican immigrants in their own country. So: building resentment, which can go both ways.

After the 2002 Bali bombings killed 202 people, the West assumed that the West was the primary target. Sure enough, the bombings were the work of Jemaah Islamiyah (JI; "Muslim Group"), an international gang seeking regional Islamist rule stretching from the Philippines all the way to Thailand.

However, I was in Bali not long after the killings, and local opinion held that Westerners could have been targeted anywhere in Indonesia (as they later were); blowing up *Bali's* most popular tourist zone also wounded Bali and its much-envied, wealthier Hindu population. Perhaps JI played a bank shot.

For what it's worth, most Balinese folks were incredibly nice, despite hurting terribly at the time. I therefore had a miserable visit, and I can't wait to go back.

KALIMANTAN

Kalimantan is the opposite of Java—so densely forested that some chunks remain completely unexplored, although international timber and mining companies are doing their best to give us a view.

Indigenous groups comprise just under half of the 9 million people here. About 2 million of these are called "Dayak" (roughly meaning "inland people"); well-known for a welcoming culture, their 100-yard longhouses have become a modern hippie retreat. However, piss them off, and machetes used for animal sacrifices find other purposes. Headhunting as a form of revenge was a Dayak tradition until the 20th century.

Unfortunately, Indonesia's willingness to sell its rain forests also sold many Dayaks' livelihood out from under them. Jakarta also decided it would be a bright idea to transplant folks from the poor, crowded areas of Java and Madura into Kalimantan. The Madurese generally did OK, rising from grinding poverty to just poverty, often as farmers or laborers in the logging industry—both of which require the very same land that Dayak traditions are built on. As a bonus, Madurese culture is itself notoriously confrontational.

So suddenly a bunch of poor damn Dayaks and poor damn Madurese found themselves tossed together like the world's most hellish episode of *Big Brother.* From 1996 to 2003, the Madurese got voted out. With machetes, spears, and torches. In 1997, about five hundred were killed, and perhaps twenty thousand were run out of town. Violence flared again in 1999 and 2000, and things culminated in 2001, when Dayaks massacred much of the town of Sampit, decapitating perhaps two hundred people.

Indonesia sent troops, and similar violence hasn't been reported since. But I can find no report of any real resolution, either.

MOLUCCAS

Religious tensions began here in the 16th century, when Portuguese colonists planted Catholicism into this mostly Islamic region. Fortunately, Moluccans developed a mediation process called *pela gandong* ("brotherhoods between villages"), allowing everybody to chat things through.

Unfortunately, Jakarta's 1970s plan to transmigrate poor Javans dumped boatloads of fresh Muslims into the region, shifting the centuries-old balance. Finally, in 1999, a Christian bus driver got into it with two Muslims after a traffic accident on the island of Ambon; the ensuing violence leapt from island to island, leading to thousands of deaths. It wasn't until 2002 that everybody remembered they pretty much worship the same god. The resulting peace agreement has generally held. So far.

SULAWESI

As in the Moluccas, Christians and Muslims in the town of Poso once had a fairly peaceful coexistence, facilitated by a power-sharing arrangement in which the governorship alternated between Christians and Muslims. Unfortunately, the same dang Javanese transmigration plan hit here, too, so in 1998, the Muslim governor broke with tradition and nominated another Muslim to succeed him. Soon, Christian and Muslim teenagers went fisty, followed by Muslim attacks, Christian retaliations, and so forth.

The death toll is over 1,500, mostly Muslims, and the near-destruction of Poso. A peace accord settled things for a while, but sporadic killings reportedly continue.

PAPUA

While Indonesia is now ostensibly a democracy, this would be news in Papua, where merely raising certain flags or speaking out on certain days can get you shot.

The Dutch didn't decolonize Papua until 1962, specifically because of Papua's gold, silver, copper, timber, oil, and other resources. When the Dutch finally tossed the ball to the UN, most Papuans planned on independence, but the deal placed the area under temporary Indonesian rule, pending an independence vote. Indonesia promptly rolled in its troops, and the vote was never held.

With Papua's Melanesian Christians estranged from Javanese Muslims by ethnicity, language, and religion, the Free Papua Movement flag began flying almost immediately. A few years of guerrilla war later, Jakarta responded by killing thousands, militarizing the province, and declaring the area off-limits to foreign journalists. Secessionist conflict has flared for almost forty-five years, always dominated by the Indonesian military.

Jakarta has meanwhile allowed a U.S. company to build the largest gold mine in the world. Papua nonetheless remains the poorest part of Indonesia. Which is saying something.

In 2001, international pressure and local resistance earned Papua more autonomy and a better cut of the resource pie. However, in 2003, Jakarta violated this agreement by declaring the western end of Papua a separate province, known as West Irian Jaya. Divide and conquer. As elsewhere, Jakarta is also shipping in boatloads of Muslims, apparently hoping to Javanize Papua into Indonesiatude.

It's hard to estimate the human cost of Indonesia's grip, since Jakarta has banned foreign reporters from the region. Australian journalists have glimpsed enough, however, to draw comparisons to East Timor, and recent years have seen a steep climb in Indonesian military actions, especially near the gargantuan gold mine. The death toll probably exceeds 100,000, and the word *genocide* is creeping into the conversation.

EAST TIMOR

- East Timor v. Indonesia; independence, 2002, but meddling continues
- East Timorese army splintered into factional fighting

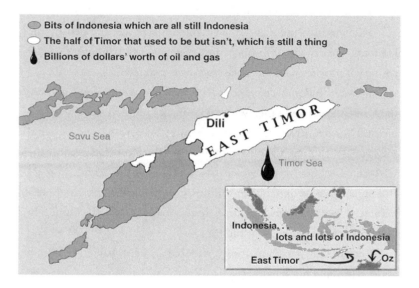

Bits of Indonesia which are all still Indonesia
The half of Timor that used to be but isn't, which is still a thing
Billions of dollars' worth of oil and gas

Dili

EAST TIMOR

Savu Sea

Timor Sea

Indonesia. . .
lots and lots of Indonesia

East Timor

Oz

Indonesia, the intestines from which East Timor hangs like an appendix, was colonized by the Netherlands, but East Timor was colonized by Portugal, so this island was split long ago. (*Timor*, incidentally, means "east." So the country is actually "East East.")

During WWII, however, all of Timor was immersed in fighting against the Japanese. The Allies took hundreds of casualties; the Japanese lost about two thousand. But fifty thousand Timorese—one in ten—died to defend their homeland. The Battle of Timor occupied an entire Japanese division, saving Allied manpower elsewhere; some historians believe it also prevented direct attacks on Australia. The Allies owe Timor big-time.

Following the war, Indonesia gained independence from the Netherlands after a guerrilla struggle, but East Timor reverted to Portugal's authoritarian rule. When Portugal began decolonization in 1974, it left a power vacuum in East Timor. Amid growing conflict, a popular socialist movement declared independence in 1975.

This lasted all of nine days.

Thousands of miles away, the United States was gripped by the Domino Theory. To wit: once one country gets communism, any country it touches will, too. Like warts. Or pink eye.

So when Indonesia's president Sukarno accepted communist aid, the United States and other Western countries instinctively allied with his rival Suharto (two letters, big difference), who rose to power amid the slaughter of more than half a million people. (No exaggeration; the CIA called it "one of the worst mass murders of the 20th century.") But Suharto's government was still shaky, so maintaining his authority became a key Western objective, lest warty, pink-eyed communist dominoes clatter throughout the Pacific.

Bottom line: what Suharto wanted, Suharto got, half a megadeath aside. Revolting but true.

When East Timorese socialists declared independence, Suharto feared that East Timor could become an ally of China or the Soviet Union, creating Indonesia's very own Cuba.

Eight days later, President Gerald Ford and Secretary of State Henry Kissinger were in Jakarta. Declassified White House documents reveal that Ford and Kissinger gave Suharto a green light to invade. "We understand the problem and the intentions you have," said the president to the dictator. "It is important that whatever you do succeeds quickly," said Kissinger. Then they talked about oil for a while. Suharto's troops poured into East Timor the next day; up to 100,000 Timorese were killed within a year.

Amnesty International puts the total deaths as a result of the occupation at 200,000—about one East Timorese in five. The U.S. and other Western nations continued arming Suharto. Two East Timorese independence leaders, meanwhile, won a Nobel Peace Prize.

Fortunately, Suharto was forced into retirement by the Cold War's end, a 1997 currency crisis, and embarrassing footage of Indonesian troops slaughtering protesters. When a UN agreement led to a vote, East Timor's public chose independence. In 2002, East Timor got its groove back.

Happy ending? Nope. Pro-Indonesian militants continued attacks, hoping to sabotage the baby nation. After UN peacekeepers forced the militias to back off, East Timor tried to pick up the pieces, but with one of the lowest per capita GDPs on earth. East Timor's entire annual budget couldn't afford the New York Yankees' starting infield.

East Timor also faces tension within its own borders. Easterners—who are therefore Eastern East Easterners, given the country's name—tend toward Papuan descent, while westerners are more Malay. In 2006, westerners in the army decided they didn't get paid as well as easterners, so some rebelled. In short, the East Timor military has split between (if I understand this right) *western* East Timorese and *eastern* East Timorese.

Well, shoot.

Worse, this sudden instability seems to have given every Timorese gang-banger with a machete and a vendetta a chance to work on his to-do list. Soon, Dili had more than one hundred buildings destroyed, thousands of Timorese fled their homes, and international peacekeepers had to roll in. Again. Meanwhile, hunger and looting. Oy.

Meanwhile, if peace ever comes, there's a buttload ("buttload": $20 billion) of gas and oil under the Timor Sea—not much to a First World country (ten stealth bombers, say), but enough cash for decades of Timorese growth. However, Australia—whose bacon the Timorese helped save, remember—signed a 1972 deal with Suharto giving

Australia two-thirds of the Timor Sea. But East Timor didn't exist yet, so they call shenanigans. If the line goes down the middle, East Timor's cut probably rises from about $4 billion to $12 billion over the next twenty years.

It's not clear how the oil issue will be resolved. We could ask the World Court, but Australia withdrew right about the time they signed the oil deal. How convenient.

THE PHILIPPINES

- NPA/Huk communist rebellion v. Manila, now with extrajudicial killings
- MILF Muslim Moro rebels v. Manila
- Abu Sayyaf Islamists v. Manila
- Six-way border conflict over Spratly Islands

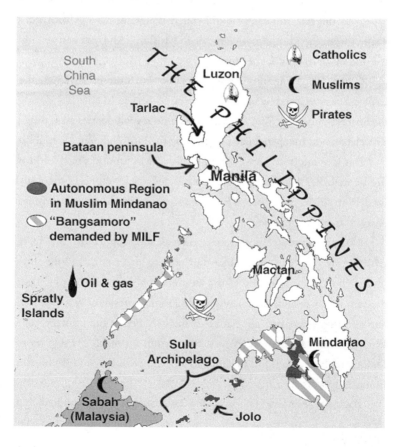

n 1521, as Hernán Cortés was stomping the Aztecs (see "Mexico," p. 156), Ferdinand Magellan arrived in the Philippines with much friendlier intentions. Naturally, *he's* the one who got a spear in the face.

Nonetheless, the Philippines became a Spanish possession, adopting Spanish names and Catholicism. However, in Mindanao and the Sulu Archipelago to the south, Malay-descended Muslims (called *Moro* by the Spanish, after the Moors back home) resisted. Eventually, Spain decided one spear in the face was enough, letting local sultans keep order. To this day, the south is still called Bangsamoro—"Moroland," distinct from the Philippines—by Moro Muslims. And you can already see one modern conflict brewing.

Come 1896, Filipinos revolted against the Spanish. In 1898, the United States attacked Spain, too, trapping its fleet in Manila Bay during the Spanish-American War. Delighted Filipino revolutionaries soon issued a Declaration of Independence proclaiming the First Philippine Republic.

But Commodore Dewey didn't sail halfway around the world for the benefit of *Filipinos*. The U.S. considered the Philippines a colony won from Spain, no more. The Filipino representative wasn't even a party to treaty negotiations.

Not surprisingly, local rebels turned their sights on the U.S., which now fought a much bloodier war to prevent the Philippines from falling into the hands of the Filipinos. At least 100,000 civilians died from war-related causes before the Filipino president was captured and compelled to swear allegiance to the U.S. before the military governor, Arthur MacArthur. (Arthur MacArthur is notable for two more reasons: (a) his name is fun to shout in an echo chamber, and (b) his son Douglas appears shortly.)

Back home, Mark Twain was so infuriated at the bloodshed that he wrote a famous protest poem. Twain was the Rage Against the Machine of his day.

Fast-forward to 1941: the Japanese arrived the day after Pearl Harbor, eventually forcing thousands of U.S. soldiers to undertake a 65-mile Death March from the Bataan Peninsula to a prison camp in Tarlac, where prisoners continued to die while Filipinos kept up resistance in the countryside. This "People's Anti-Japanese Army" (the "Huks," from a contraction of the Filipino name) was Marxist, but the U.S. didn't mind, given that they were the enemy of the enemy. However, once WWII was over, the U.S. maintained their naval and air bases here—specifically to *fight* communism. So, again, the U.S. confronted their former allies. Tens of thousands of Huks died in the rebellion.

In the early 1970s, the Philippine government was faced with (a) a fresh Huk rebellion called the New People's Army (NPA), thriving on Chinese supplies, and (b) a Muslim group called the Moro National Liberation Front (MNLF) firing up in the south. In 1972, President Ferdinand Marcos declared martial law, after which he ruled essentially as a dictator for life. Marcos's crackdown drove thousands of additional recruits into the NPA, whose guerrilla war continues to this day.

Marcos ran the Philippines as a fiefdom, imprisoning opponents, torturing dissidents, and looting billions. The U.S. looked the other way, given Marcos's anticommunism.

Marcos's leading rival was Benigno Aquino, the telegenic scion of a powerful political family. A vigorous liberal who achieved office at an early age, Aquino's golden boy status was enhanced by his lovely, talented, equally high-bred wife. (JFK much? Just wait.) Unfortunately, Aquino spent most of his life after 1972 in prison.

In 1978, while still imprisoned, Aquino founded the People Power Party, which would have achieved power had the elections been remotely honest. But in 1980, he suffered a serious heart attack and was rushed to a hospital in Dallas, Texas, after which he moved to Massachusetts and accepted a fellowship from Harvard. However, Aquino soon returned to the Philippines, hoping to work for peaceful change.

Landing amid heavy "protection" provided by Marcos, our Filipino JFK was shot five seconds after he stepped off the plane. To this day, the shooter isn't positively known, although a fall guy was instantly found and shot to death. Amid conspiracy theories, the Marcos government appointed a high-level commission whose findings are still in doubt. If Kevin Costner can do a Filipino accent, Oliver Stone has another three-hour movie.

Incidentally, the priest who presided over Aquino's funeral was named Cardinal Sin. That's just fun to know.

Aquino's death galvanized opposition to Marcos, and by 1986, the dictator, his stolen billions, his wife Imelda, and her pricey shoes were whisked away by a U.S. helicopter to live out their days in Hawaii. Aquino's widow, Corazon, became president, *Time* named her Woman of the Year, rainbows fell from the sky, and bird poop smelled like mint from then on.

If only. After all, there were still two major insurrections under way.

Aquino initiated peace talks with the Moro rebels, who agreed to elections throughout all Moro-claimed territories. The result: the Autonomous Region in Muslim Mindanao, a self-governing area about as "independent" as Québec is from Canada. But the MNLF got to be in charge, so hey. However, a more radical faction, the Moro Islamic Liberation Front (MILF), wasn't satisfied, so peace is still a ways off.

By the way, no respectable writer would ever digress into musing on the acronym MILF, picturing a violent Islamist insurgency with a soft, full bosom, baking cookies in a too-short skirt, licking the spoon slooooowly, and smiling a naughty, naughty smile. That would be completely irresponsible.

Further complicating things: Abu Sayyaf, a group of Islamist rebels based around Jolo and the surrounding islands. Abu Sayyaf seeks an Islamic state stretching from the Philippines to Malaysia, Indonesia, southern Thailand, and clear the hell to Burma. All they need now is to defeat five governments. Nice to see religious fanatics setting realistic goals.

Abu Sayyaf is tight with Indonesia's Jemaah Islamiyah (see "Indonesia," p. 132) and Al-Qaeda in general. How tight? One of Abu Sayyaf's favorite ideas, Bojinka, involved (a) the conversion of multiple passenger jets into large flying bombs, and (b) attacking buildings in the United States, plotted in part by (c) Khalid Shaikh Mohammed. Sound familiar?* The Philippine army has killed a bunch of Abu Sayyaf big shots recently, but this one's a long way from over.

As to the communist NPA, Aquino's successor, Fidel Ramos, made surprising progress in talks, and after 1998, a peace process was under way. But after 9-11, the U.S. and the European Union, now suddenly terror-focused, deemed the NPA a terrorist organization, which made continued negotiations politically difficult for the new government of Gloria Arroyo. (Granted, the NPA *is* extremely violent. But while the "terrorist" label here is accurate, using it has demonstrably led to more killings.) And during the Arroyo years, unfortunately, democracy in the Philippines has come somewhat undone. Her 2004 reelection, in which she narrowly defeated a high-school dropout, is increasingly viewed as fraudulent, and after her 2006 "State of Emergency" declaration, warrantless arrests and extrajudicial killings returned.

At this writing, the Philippines are a bad place to be a peace activist, liberal clergy member, or labor leader. Anything that might be stretched into NPA sympathies—including mere opposition to the hundreds of killings of activists—could bring you a visit from two nice men in ski masks on a motorcycle.

---

*Bojinka was uncovered in 1995, and Mohammed was indicted on federal charges in New York state in 1996. After 9-11, however, the White House would repeatedly insist that no one could have foreseen an attack.

There's also a small, brewing border conflict with six other countries over the Spratly Islands, under which large oil and natural gas deposits probably exist. So throw Taiwan, Vietnam, Malaysia, Brunei, and especially China into the mix. But that's more of a long-term headache.

Finally, the extreme poverty of Moro lands, added to cultural factors and a lack of faith in civil politics, has resulted in a resurgence of sea piracy. *Ahrr.* So that's an extra thrill for your vacation.

That's not to say the Philippines aren't a fine place to visit. Mactan, where Magellan was killed, is now home to the country's second-biggest airport. Millions of visitors arrive every year for snorkeling and scuba. Very few get spears in the face anymore.

AMERICAS

COLOMBIA

- Two competing left-wing insurgencies v. army, militias, and U.S.-backed government
- Most parties involved in cocaine trade; drug barons lean right

Since the Spanish showed up in 1525, Colombia has offered the world gold, silver, platinum, oil, coal, emeralds, coffee, bananas, sugar, cotton, stunning beaches, and Shakira. In a saner world, Colombia would be phenomenally wealthy.

Pro-union liberals ruled Colombia starting in the 1930s, but conservatives took power after WWII. In 1948, this factional split led to a full-out civil war ("La Violencia"), killing up to 300,000 Colombians. A peace agreement in 1958 healed things between the two elite parties, but banned everyone else from politics. This just rearranged the problem, and rebellion soon arose from the rural disenfranchised.

Ever since, Colombia has resembled a forty-year-long tag-team cage match between these two sides:

1) a left-wing insurgency, but with two competing groups, versus
2) the government, often in cooperation with a right-wing counterinsurgency.

On the left, the National Liberation Army (ELN) was founded by Marxist intellectuals and liberation theologists. ("Liberation theology" views the Gospels as democratizing, even socialist. Extremists take this one step further, deciding "the meek shall inherit the earth" with semi-automatic weapons.) Their rival is the Revolutionary Armed Forces of Colombia (FARC), founded by hard-line communists and peasants braced for armed struggle. If violent Colombian leftists are the Odd Couple, ELN is Felix and FARC is Oscar. You can also remember their

151

locations by applying an unfair U.S. stereotype, with self-righteous intellectuals in the north and well-armed peasants in the south.

ELN often targets foreign oil companies; FARC is more about hijackings and assassinations, often for financial instead of political goals. Both groups are also in the kidnapping business; FARC has held some victims for years at a time.

FARC is one of the largest rebel groups on earth, 15,000 strong, and often able to attack almost anywhere in the country. The Colombian government ceded them a chunk of territory the size of Switzerland for a while, although that didn't bring peace. FARC also rakes in half a billion dollars a year from cocaine, most of it heading up U.S. noses. ELN long frowned on the drug trade, given the moralism mixed into its violence, so lacking the extra capital, ELN lost mindshare, falling to about 4,000 members. FARC and right-wing groups may eventually run ELN out of business.

On the right, Colombia has also suffered since 1997 under the United Self-Defense Forces of Colombia (AUC), a confederation of local militias financed by landowners, drug lords, and military generals. AUC functions almost as a national brand, with vigilantes in each community joining as local agents: structurally, think of Amway with guns.

AUC has shed far more blood than the other groups combined, killing not just armed rebels, but union and peasant leaders, human rights activists, and progressive politicians. Thanks to AUC's habit of attacking whole villages suspected of supporting lefties—even if sometimes their only "crime" is labor, peace, or environmental activism— over 3 million Colombians have been displaced.

However, since AUC has been tight with rightists in the Colombian government—who were in turn allied with Washington, always eager to squish rebel commies—the United States waited until 2003 to list AUC as the big bad boys they are.

All this was complicated in the 1980s by the growth of cocaine as

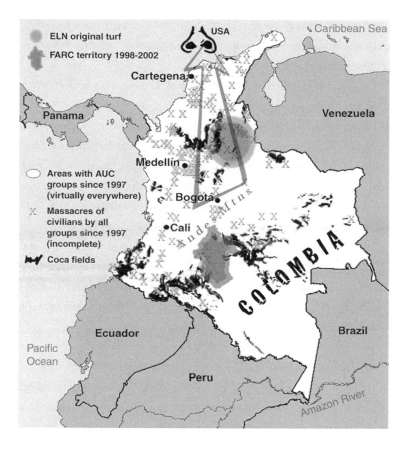

ELN original turf

FARC territory 1998-2002

USA

Caribbean Sea

Cartegena

Panama

Venezuela

Medellín

Areas with AUC
groups since 1997
(virtually everywhere)

X Massacres of
civilians by all
groups since 1997
(incomplete)

Coca fields

Bogotá

Cali

Andes Mtns.

COLOMBIA

Ecuador

Pacific
Ocean

Brazil

Peru

Amazon River

Colombia's biggest moneymaker. Since it's illegal, it's controlled only by whoever holds the guns where it's grown, processed, and shipped. So we've also got a fifth faction—drug lords armed to the nads, usually (but not always) siding with the army, cops, and the paramilitaries.

The United States has armed the Colombian government with billions' worth of weapons over the years, none of it significantly slowing the flow of blow. "Plan Colombia" was a Clinton-era solution, spraying herbicides on coca fields at a cost of $4.7 billion. This made a minor dent in cultivation, but did little to the overall trade. (Supply and demand: leave demand in place, cut supply, and the price increases. The commodity becomes more profitable per unit, creating *greater* incentive to manufacture it.)

Colombia's current president, Álvaro Uribe, won reelection in 2006 after his troops pushed FARC out of most major cities. Thanks to Uribe, it's no longer insane to vacation in Colombia, as long as you fly between cities and keep your head down. Tourism is surging, and major cruise lines now visit Cartagena. With luck, tourist cash may further diminish the appeal of insurgency. On the other hand, an entire Carnival Cruise ship may be taken hostage someday, with Kathie Lee Gifford aboard. Either way, something good happens.

In the countryside, however, there's no real end in sight. To the good, the government and ELN are in peace talks, and thousands of AUC members have demobilized under an amnesty program that offers them job training, health insurance, and two years of employment in exchange for not killing people anymore. Sweet deal.

However, for some of AUC's leadership, negotiations also seem to be a way for drug lords to negotiate retirement with impunity. Of AUC's ten negotiators, eight are targets of U.S. drug enforcement. Meanwhile, recent press reports implicate several of Uribe's associates in illegal ties to the paramilitaries, so the government is still mixed up with AUC and vice versa.

Bottom line: ELN hasn't quit, AUC is still in business, and FARC remains a drug-fueled monster. Not to mention a few independent drug lords and militias freelancing around.

Reading Colombian newspapers as I write this—and in Colombia, the press usually isn't so much transparent as it is bullet-ridden, letting you peek through the holes—a FARC attack in the town of Meta has just killed fifteen soldiers, some AUC guys have been assassinated in Medellín, and FARC has killed two women in Angostura.

In Nicaragua, meanwhile, police have just seized a full *ton* of cocaine from a Colombian boat bound for the U.S. A big bust? Hardly. That's about *one day* of American nose candy. Colombia produces 80 percent of the world's cocaine; the U.S. consumes more than half. In a real sense, the U.S. government sends military force into one side of antidrug efforts, while the sinus cavities of U.S. citizens send boatloads of cash to the other.

MEXICO

- Chiapas rebellion, now a local de facto government
- Border friction with the United States
- General strike and seizure of the capital of Oaxaca, 2006
- Drug war intensifying nationwide

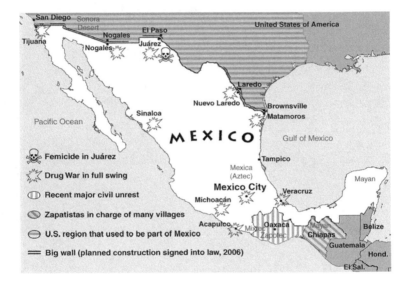

Aztecs ruled here for centuries, although their reign was less an empire than a protection racket: Mixtecs, Zapotecs, and other neighbors could go about their lives as long as they didn't make trouble and paid tribute under threat of violence.

Thus enriched, the Aztecs developed music, poetry, and rituals to keep the sun moving—we owe them for that big-time—but in 1519, Spanish colonists commanded by Hernán Cortés arrived at a settlement they named Veracruz before pushing into the Aztec capital of Tenochtitlán.

The Spaniards carried guns and smallpox; the latter was worse.

The indigenous population dropped 75 to 90 percent within one human lifetime. The Spanish also built a new capital, Mexico City, pretty much where Tenochtitlán was, shoved the surviving locals into feudal oppression, and imported slaves from Africa. Power correlated with skin tone in a fairly continuous spectrum.

After Spain's empire became overextended, a ten-year war starting in 1810 led to Mexican independence. Mexico abolished slavery, pissing off slaveholders in the part of Mexico we now call Texas, who then started their own revolution. Nobody at the Alamo mentions this, but at least some Texans were fighting for freedom . . . *to keep slaves.* Then again, the rest of the U.S. south did the same thing later, so we can't act too surprised. In 1836, Texas won independence, re-legalized slavery, and made everybody happy. Except the slaves.

Texas wanted to join the U.S., partly to get help in keeping the Mexicans out—some things never change—and in 1845 they got their wish over Mexico's strident objections. President Polk saw Mexican outrage as an opportunity, and in 1846 he sent U.S. troops into disputed territory as a provocation. "Mr. Polk's War" was denounced by Congressman Abraham Lincoln and Henry David Thoreau, but it was one of the most successful wars of conquest ever. After a landing at Veracruz followed by a march to the capital (history doesn't just repeat itself; sometimes it screams), the U.S. gained virtually all of Mexico's territory north of the current border, including not just all of Texas, but California, Nevada, and Utah, plus major chunks of Arizona, New Mexico, Colorado, and Wyoming. Counting Texas, Mexico lost about half of itself, and the U.S. swelled by about 50 percent in less than two years.

In the U.S., however, war supporters' experience of using military force to get exactly what they wanted helped lead to the horrific U.S. Civil War. So even the winners paid a heavy price.

Mexico City was administered by a U.S. general named Win Scott, but the government was chronically shaky. Liberalization was followed by French occupation, homegrown dictatorship, a revolution, civil war, and finally (we're up to 1930 now) a troubled republic run by the Institutional Revolutionary Party (PRI), which ran things for about sixty years. The idea that Revolution could become Institutional tells you what follows.

PRI rule was increasingly oppressive, including a 1968 slaughter so gross that the Interior Minister was later charged with genocide. The

U.S. didn't blink; both nations feared Latin American revolution, so the Mexican government allowed the FBI to operate on its soil, and Mexico City became home to the largest CIA station outside U.S. territory. (The Mexico City CIA chief was coincidentally *also* named Win Scott. History screams once again.) According to declassified documents, two Mexican presidents were CIA informants. In practice, that meant only that the CIA was reliant on Mexico's very top bullshitters. But still.

A Mexican protester labels herself: "100% cannon fodder."

Corruption and a growing drug trade spurred each other along. The latter has led to violence that now kills more than two thousand people each year; thirty thousand government troops are currently occupied in an ongoing battle★ with a half-dozen cartels working with their Colombian counterparts to feed North American appetites (see "Colombia," p. 151). Toss in economic and racial inequality, and by the late 20th century, a large underclass had few options. So millions of Mexicans headed north seeking work, despite

---

★At least one cartel's private army has reportedly included numerous former members of Mexican and Guatemalan Special Forces (see "Central America," p. 165); these men would be both better trained and better paid than most of the government's own troops.

obvious friction. The U.S. has responded by spending tens of billions trying to control the world's most-crossed border via infrared surveillance, aerial drones, and pissed-off Arizonans with rifles and lawn chairs. Nonetheless, a million people still cross illegally each year. The Sonoran Desert will soon get a vast wall with all the trimmings, but mountainous border areas will remain unfenced—areas you'd attempt only if you were, um, *desperate*. We may soon find out exactly what that word means.

On the Mexican side of the border, factories sprang up where Mexicans work crazy hours for low wages, with the profits heading back to U.S. (or other multinational) corporations. The North American Free Trade Agreement (NAFTA) was advocated to change things, but the border still contains pockets of Third World right next to the First.★

One unintended result of NAFTA: rebellion in Chiapas, where Mayan farmers saw NAFTA's scrapping of protective tariffs as a major economic threat. The very day NAFTA took effect, a masked man called "Subcomandante Marcos" (actually Rafael Guillén, a philosophy professor from Tampico, but *shhh*—don't tell) led an uprising by the Zapatistas, named for a famous Mexican revolutionary.

After a brief skirmish, a truce began that has held for almost fifteen years. The Subcomandante (who now prefers "Delegate Zero"— OK, Rafael, what*ever*) has become a national figure, and the Zapatistas even have their own blog. The revolution may not be televised, but you can stream it in QuickTime.

Just up the road, Oaxaca has lots of rural Mixtecs and Zapotecs, and rural teachers have often staged a near annual strike in Oaxaca's

---

★Since 1993, more than four hundred young women, many of whom came to work in these factories, have been abducted and murdered in and around Ciudad Juárez amid a climate of stunning impunity. Open season on working-class women may be slowing due to increasing public attention, but most of the killings may never be solved.

main square to get the governor to cough up a decent wage. However, in 2004, a career PRI man named Ulises Ruíz became governor amid charges of electoral fraud. In 2006, the teachers refused to recognize his authority, so Ruíz sent in three thousand cops. Soon, the protest wasn't about wages; it was about Ruíz. Protesters took control of the town, and Ruíz retreated to Mexico City.

Eventually, however, thousands of federal police poured in. Hundreds of protesters were soon arrested, and the town square has been repainted, as if to rub a giant eraser across Oaxaca. A friend who lives there says it's a literal whitewashing—months of protest, magically wiped away. It's an illusion, of course. Oaxacans remember.

But for now, the government atop Tenochtitlán is allowing Mixtecs and Zapotecs to go about their lives in peace, as long as they don't make trouble and pay their taxes under threat of violence.

History screams.

HAITI

- Multifactional violence, albeit with some classic left-right features

Cuba

Atlantic Ocean

◯ Areas where the Spanish
never found giant
assloads of gold

$\mathcal{H} \mathcal{A} I T I$

Dominican
Republic

Port-au-Prince

◖ Countries that still have trees
◗ Hostile ground for Haitians

Caribbean Sea

n 1942, Christopher Columbus arrived on the northwest
coast. Things have arguably gone downhill ever since.

Once Columbus convinced himself there was *gold! massive,
magnificent, glorious gold!*, native Tainos got a faceful of slavery and
smallpox. Once they were thinned out—one generation—the
Spanish imported African slaves, sending them to look for *gold! spectacular, beautiful assloads of gold!*, which they never found.

When Spain moved on, the French moved in. Their colony
prospered, despite burning through even more African slaves. The
Africans outnumbered the French 10 to 1, but were kept in such

horrid conditions that they usually died before doing much about it. But in 1791, the slaves rose up. It took a while, but eventually Napoleon's troops got yellow fever, the Africans kicked butt, and in 1804, Haití became an independent nation.

Not surprisingly, everybody who wanted to *keep* slavery was immediately hostile. And remember, this was sixty years before slavery ended in the United States, so Haiti-inspired rebellions pissed off U.S. slaveowners no end. Blockades, isolation, and instability followed.

As WWI cued up, Woodrow Wilson secured the U.S. southern border by occupying Haiti, imposing a constitution (written by FDR, or so he claimed), and instituting what became decades of heavy-duty social engineering. The U.S. also seized the Haitian government's modest gold reserves. Columbus would have been envious.

The U.S. restructuring of Haiti was a mixed bag: better schools and health care v. centralized control, disrupting much social fabric. Plus, the threat of rebellion—nobody likes an occupier—led the U.S. to create Haiti's National Guard, which the dictators François "Papa Doc" and Jean-Claude "Baby Doc" Duvalier would later use to violently consolidate power. However, the U.S. looked the other way; communist Cuba was next door, and one thing the Duvaliers manifestly *weren't* was communist.

Under the Duvaliers, things went from bad to insane. Given its resources, Haiti could have become a prosperous, peaceful nation. By the time Baby Doc was overthrown in 1986, Haiti was almost completely deforested, 80 percent of Haitians lived in poverty, and political violence was enshrined as a fact of life. Haiti has now been the poorest country in the hemisphere since long before most current Haitians were born.

The following years have some classic Third World features: a Duvalier-style right-wing elite has been massively outnumbered by the poor but generally supported by corporate interests, who reflexively refer to Third World countries as "labor forces" and "markets," even when almost nobody has a job or can buy anything much.

In 1991, a populist movement brought to power a left-wing Catholic priest named Jean-Bertrand Aristide, who openly denounced U.S. involvement. Aristide was soon deposed by a junta whose paramilitaries were originally funded by U.S. intelligence. However, a flood of refugees fleeing the junta attempted to reach Florida, and the domestic political fallout forced President Clinton to change course. U.S. Marines reinstated Aristide on the explicit condition that he drop his radical agenda, embrace a World Bank deal to invite foreign investment, and leave office the next year. When Aristide left on schedule, it was the first peaceful, sorta democratic transition in Haiti's history.

Out of office, Aristide returned to his more radical positions and ran for office again in 2000. After a disputed vote, both sides swore in their own government, and the instability screwed the fragile chances for international investment. The economy fell apart again, and violence erupted from all sides, with sheer criminality and petty loyalties frequently obscuring any right-left political context. By 2004, the opposition controlled two northern cities and were marching on the capital. Aristide soon flew into exile. Whether he was removed by U.S. troops or left voluntarily depends on if you believe (a) Aristide or (b) Dick Cheney.

The political heirs of the Duvaliers then did their thing, cracking down on the rebellious slums. Gangs of former military men staged thousands of score-settling murders with total impunity; the medical journal *Lancet* estimated eight thousand in Port-au-Prince alone.

Why don't more Haitians flee to the Dominican Republic? Because the reception toward Haitians makes the U.S. view of Mexicans seem downright affectionate. The Dominican government makes it almost impossible for a Haitian to naturalize or receive health care, housing, or education. And with Haiti's violence, some Dominicans feel justified in attacking Haitians in preemptive self-defense. According to Amnesty International, mob violence is not uncommon, usually near the border.

Why don't Haitians there just go back to Haiti? Maybe because it's *Haiti*.

Eventually, the UN sent peacekeepers, and (fast-forwarding through more carnage and another messy election) Haiti again has a pretty-much-elected president, René Préval. So far, Préval is pursuing both international investment and outright aid from the U.S., Cuba, Venezuela, France, and anyone willing to talk. If you have a bank, an oil company, or twenty bucks to spare, Préval will want to chat.

There's still loads of violence and impunity. Your average Cuban makes twice as much income as a typical Haitian. In a country ravaged by HIV and malnutrition, there's one physician for every twenty thousand people. Literacy sits around 50 percent. Infant mortality is fifteen times higher than in most developed countries. Between low life expectancy and the exodus of adults to the U.S. and elsewhere, the median age is only eighteen.

It's not clear how much can change under Préval, whose own program to get Haiti back on track will take twenty-five years. Best case.

CENTRAL AMERICA

I n Central America's last quarter century, five nations have seen hot wars, three have endured death tolls in the six figures, and one has suffered a genocide.

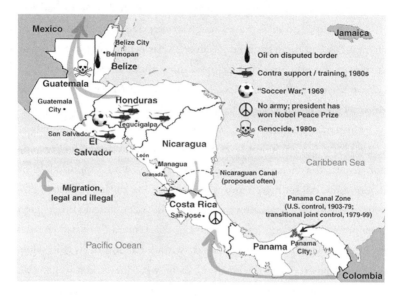

BELIZE

- No war; just don't get killed

The former British Honduras is best known as a tourist playground; Belize City's astronomical murder rate doesn't echo in the posh coastal villas of Ambergris Caye.

However, Guatemala long claimed Belize as its easternmost province (which it once was under Spanish rule), recognizing Belizean sovereignty only in 1991. The border is still disputed, and the 2006 discovery of commercial quantities of light sweet crude oil on the Belizean side may intensify things. Vacationers will probably never notice.

GUATEMALA

- Rightist dictatorship v. left-wing insurgency (1960s–90s)
- Genocide of indigenous Mayans

Guatemala is home to descendants of the ancient Mayans recently eulogized by Mel Gibson's *Apocalypto,* although real Mayans had less arterial spurting, no mass graves, and a stricter obedience to the laws of physics. Also, in the Mayan era (as ever), solar eclipses could not occur during a full moon; real Mayans knew more about astronomy than Mel Gibson seems to. In short, *Apocalypto* may be to Mayan history what *Attack of the Killer Tomatoes* is to salad.

Guatemala spent the early 20th century built around the interests of United Fruit (now Chiquita), its biggest landowner. But a 1944 revolution led to the election of Juan José Arévalo, who supported labor unions, universal suffrage, and workers' rights. His successor, Jacobo Arbenz, went further, legalizing the communist party (among others) and attempting a clever land reform: claiming that United Fruit had cheated on its taxes by pretending its land was worth a fraction of its true value, Arbenz proposed to buy the land for exactly what they said it was worth.

To Washington, this might as well have been a Soviet invasion. The newly formed CIA set up a propaganda apparatus to freak out the locals, hooked up rightist Col. Carlos Castillo Armas with some half-competent rebels . . . and lucked out. Although Armas's men got their butts kicked at first, Arbenz's generals believed a full-scale U.S. invasion was imminent, so they weenied out. Armas, the CIA, and United Fruit were in.

Guatemalan democracy—still called "The Ten Years of Spring"—was out. Armas revamped the secret police, jailed thousands, rescinded land reforms, and implemented Central America's first death squad. The CIA gave Armas lists of suspected communists, many of whom were summarily executed.

After Armas himself was murdered—you saw *that* coming—left-wing military officers formed several underground guerrilla organizations. In response, right-wing militias tortured and killed anyone suspected of guerrilla sympathies, especially students and the rural poor. Rebel attacks on the capital convinced the United States to reinforce the Guatemalan government. By 1966, declassified documents show that U.S. State Department officials had set up the presidential palace itself as a "safe house" for Guatemalan security forces who implemented "kidnapping, torture . . . bombings, street assassinations, and executions."

A 1982 coup led Efraín Ríos Montt, an Evangelical who felt chosen by his god, to the presidency. Ríos Montt dismantled the constitution and congress, then unleashed a righteous fury—including torture, assassination, and mass murder of indigenous Mayans, whom Ríos Montt stereotyped as communist sympathizers.

"The guerrilla is the fish," Ríos Montt said. "The people are the sea. If you cannot catch the fish, you have to drain the sea." Saddam Hussein was hanged for the same thing.

President Reagan visited Guatemala City at the height of the bloodshed, proclaiming Ríos Montt as "a man of great personal integrity," "totally dedicated to democracy." On *that very day*—December 4, 1982—fifty-eight of Ríos Montt's commandos flew to a camp near a village named Dos Erres, which they suspected of guerrilla sympathies.

On December 6, the soldiers ordered everyone out of their homes, conducted a lengthy search, and found no evidence of guerrilla activity. After contacting their superiors by radio, the soldiers dealt with the "suspects" individually: torturing them, killing them, and finally throwing their bodies down the village's well. One by one. Almost the *entire town*. The remains of 162 people—men and women, children and elderly—were found in that well.

This was not an aberration. In 1999, a nine-volume UN report documented over 40,000 separate human-rights violations, including more than 600 massacres of civilians. Virtually all of these atrocities were committed by the army or its allied death squads. The death toll is usually estimated at over 200,000. This happened before, during, and after the presidential visit. Thirty-four days after Dos Erres, Reagan lifted a ban on military aid to Guatemala.

A 1999 UN study concluded that the U.S. knowingly supported brutality against the Mayans that rose to the level of "acts of genocide." President Bill Clinton came close to an official apology: "Support for military forces and intelligence units which engaged in violence and widespread repression was wrong," he said. But notice that he used the passive voice, never explaining why it happened or who was responsible.

Cold warriors sometimes rationalize all this by postulating a Soviet menace that would have been worse. But not long after the 1954 coup, the CIA sent down a team of analysts, hoping to justify the invasion by proving that Arbenz was a Soviet puppet. After amassing over 150,000 pages in their document file, they came up with . . . nada.

NICARAGUA

- United States v. Nicaraguan socialists, on and off for over a century

Nicaragua's 19th century saw civil wars between elites in León and Granada (see map, p. 165), punctuated by a 1855 takeover by an American fanatic named William Walker.

Walker was a true genius, earning his first degree at age fourteen and practicing medicine before most of his peers had seen a girl naked. More important, Walker was a thrilling loon. His all-consuming life goal: to colonize Central America. Personally. (*What are we doing tomorrow night?* Pinky asks. *The same thing we do every night,* Brain replies.)

At the time, shipping magnate Cornelius Vanderbilt controlled the overland route through Nicaragua, which was the Panama Canal of its day. Given Nicaragua's instability, Vanderbilt bankrolled Walker, hoping his mercenaries could control things. Sure enough, they kicked the Nicaraguan army's butt, and President Franklin Pierce, an agreeable alcoholic excited by tales of expansionist glory, recognized Walker's group as Nicaragua's legitimate government. *Ta-da!*

Walker then sought competing bids for the use of the routes under his control. But when Vanderbilt learned Walker was taking money from competitors, Vanderbilt was livid—he'd bought Nicaragua *fair and square,* dammit. So Vanderbilt withdrew his support, cutting the puppet strings, and pumped cash into stabilizing the surrounding countries. Walker was toast.

Still, Nicaragua remained a vital transshipment point for U.S. goods, so Walker's role was eventually filled by U.S. Marines. Resistance grew around Augusto Sandino, whose guerrilla war made him a hero to lefties, although peaceniks have no hero here; his official seal showed a farmer about to dismember a U.S. Marine with a machete.

Sandino was executed by Nicaragua's U.S.-trained National Guard, headed by Anastasio Somoza, who went on to rule Nicaragua for more than twenty years. In 1956, Somoza was fatally shot by a poet, proving that the gun is mightier than the pen. One of Somoza's sons, also named Anastasio, became the new dictator. Nicaragua clearly needed more poets.

Anastasio II: *The Legend of Curly's Gold* was much like his father, except for a wider mean streak and a West Point degree. Somoza was a guest at JFK's inaugural ball and supported the subsequent U.S. invasion of Cuba, cementing his long-term U.S. alliance.

However, when a 1972 earthquake left 300,000 people homeless, Somoza's National Guard looted, hogged relief aid, and imprisoned hungry protesters. Rebellion was inevitable; the main faction, the Sandinistas, were named for Sandino, the Somozas' old enemy.

After uprisings in every major town and roughly 50,000 dead, Somoza was overthrown in 1979. His fortune was estimated at half a billion dollars, largely sucked from a country where the average annual income was under $300.

"Sandino lives."

The Sandinistas' most visible leader was Daniel Ortega, a convicted bank robber who had received Cuban support since his release. Other leaders included business and civic figures, plus Violeta Chamorro, whose husband had been assassinated for publishing *La Prensa,* an anti-Somoza newspaper. However, as Ortega's faction seized increasing power, other members resigned in disgust. Chamorro's *La Prensa* soon became as anti-Sandinista as it had been anti-Somoza, earning it CIA financial support.

Cuban assistance flowed to Ortega's government, and Soviet aid was offered. The U.S. covert response began under President Carter, but the Reagan administration escalated things: crippling sanctions, illegal mines in Nicaragua's harbors, and a rebel Contra army formed from remnants of Somoza's National Guard. The Contras were never a viable invasion force, but they were great at destroying crops, energy facilities, schools, bridges, clinics, and innocent lives. By late 1984, the Contras had rendered 150,000 people homeless. Reagan praised these men as "the moral equivalent of our founding fathers."

Reagan also claimed the Sandinistas were just a two-day drive from invading Texas. Despite being lunacy (unless a Third World army really might rush across 1,400 miles of crap roads through three countries, unimpeded, in just 48 hours, only to launch a suicidal attack on a nuclear power), this cast the Contra war as self-defense, an essential delusion.

After Congress banned Contra aid, the Contras were funded by Saudi Arabia, Israel, and arms-for-hostages deals with Iran, although Reagan later insisted, "we did not—repeat, did *not*—trade weapons or anything else for hostages." Which is exactly what they'd done. In 1986, the World Court ordered the U.S. to pay Nicaragua billions in restitution. The White House ignored the verdict.

By 1990, Nicaragua's population was exhausted enough to vote for the Stay Puft Marshmallow Man if he came with agricultural credits. The new president: Violeta Chamorro, the publisher of *La Prensa*. A fragile peace began, greatly helped by the lifting of U.S. sanctions. However, the end of Sandinista land reform led to confusion, utility prices skyrocketed, and many farmers lost their land. Meanwhile, the U.S. turned its attentions to a loud noise in Kuwait.

Today, Nicaragua is the second-poorest country in the Americas (after Haiti); about half of Nicaraguans live in poverty. Up to a million now work in Costa Rica, many illegally.

One suggested salvation: a Nicaraguan Canal, just four hundred years after it was first proposed. The idea is to build something huge enough to handle ships too big for Panama, ignore the ecological disaster, and get today's Cornelius Vanderbilts to pay for it all. However, Panama plans to upgrade its canal, which has the advantage of actually existing.

COSTA RICA

- A nice rest break

A thriving democracy whose president, Óscar Arias, has won the Nobel Peace Prize, Costa Rica has more teachers than soldiers. Its protected forests make it a popular stop for green-leaning gringos looking to find their inner howler monkey. There's small friction with the increasing number of Nicaraguan workers, but we just covered that. Onward.

EL SALVADOR

- Leftist rebels v. rightist government, army and death squads (peace deal, 1992)

Like Guatemala, El Salvador evolved as a two-tiered system of have-lands and have-land-nots, replacing bananas with coffee. The "fourteen families" (more like fifty, actually) basically ran everything, and a nasty police apparatus kept the rabble in line. A 1932 rebellion led by Farabundo Martí was crushed, killing twenty to thirty thousand; this is still known as La Matanza, "The Massacre." Dictatorship was the order of things until 1979.

A 1969 skirmish with Honduras, the "Soccer War," wasn't caused *by* the match, but by post-game tensions over dislocated Salvadoran workers on the border. Thousands died in a raging stalemate. El Salvador's impoverished air force even dropped bombs by hand.

1970s opposition coalesced in the Christian Democratic Party (PDC) led by José Napoleón Duarte. The PDC was soon stomped, and Duarte fled, but a 1979 coup gave Duarte another chance. By then, however, the left had given up on civil politics and the right had given up on allowing the left to live, so Duarte struggled. A much-needed land reform pissed off the landowners (still allied with rightists in the military) and helped kill the export economy. Twelve years of civil war followed, with the left-wing Farabundo Martí National Liberation Front (FMLN) facing the army, the right-wing Nationalist Republican Alliance (ARENA), and death squads tight with landowners.

The U.S. supported the government with advisors and $4 billion, asserting that the FMLN was the greater of two evils, but the UN later figured that over 95 percent of human rights violations were committed by the army or the ARENA-allied death squads. So toss another 75,000 bodies on the fire, including a few U.S. nuns and Archbishop

Óscar Romero, who was shot 36 days after calling on the United States not to finance these killings.

For a while, the U.S. ambassador was named, of all things, William Walker. Total coincidence can be a complete bastard.

ARENA eventually won the presidency, but rightist atrocities became an international embarrassment. Eventually, the U.S. suspended aid, and in 1992, the FMLN and ARENA signed an accord that has actually held up. The military has been slowly cleaned of human rights abusers, an amnesty is in place for crimes by both sides, and grants of land are getting many combatants invested in a nonviolent future.

Unfortunately, the civil war wrecked the agricultural economy, forcing many Salvadorans to abandon the countryside. Unable to accommodate all the newcomers, some areas of San Salvador have developed a virtual social class of gangs and hardened criminals. Migration has also turned north in a big way; about one-tenth of Salvadorans now live in the United States, and the cash they send home has become key to El Salvador's economy.

Hoping to attract more cash from abroad, the government has recently begun promoting tourism, especially along the country's beautiful Pacific coast. In turn, some former guerrillas have begun making a living by escorting visitors around the scenes of notorious massacres. Many foreign tourists prefer the beach.

HONDURAS

- Sideshow to the Contra war

Honduras also evolved as a banana republic, with U.S. rivals Standard Fruit and United Fruit (Dole and Chiquita, basically) reigning for decades as the real power behind a dazzling array of elected toadies, acting presidents, and chairmen of provisional juntas. Honduras had four different presidents in 1919 alone. By the 1950s, Honduran democracy had been dysfunctional for a generation. A 1963 military coup finished the job, and elections disappeared until the 1980s.

By then, the United States was focused on reversing the Sandinistas' control over Nicaragua, so Honduras became a staging ground for the CIA's Contra army. U.S. military aid suddenly increased by a factor of about twenty, radically militarizing Honduran life.

One sticking point: the U.S. ambassador warned of "increasing evidence of officially sponsored/sanctioned assassinations." No problem; the U.S. just changed ambassadors. Reagan's man for the job was John Negroponte,★ who gave carte blanche to the military's intelligence division (the "G-2") and secret police (the National Investigations Directorate, or DNI). The inevitable result: a surge in the kidnapping, torture, and murder of leftists, political rivals, and opponents of the Contra project.

Hundreds of Honduran civilians were killed by the CIA-trained "Battalion 3-16," whose name has reportedly become a verbal shorthand for brutality. Negroponte insisted throughout that none of this was actually happening, despite (or perhaps because of) his frequent meetings with Honduran officials later implicated in the killings.

Despite the end of the Nicaraguan war, Honduran society has yet to fully shake off the twin distortions of banana republic status and the Contra period. While the military has been placed largely under civilian control and democratic-style elections are held on schedule, the remnants of Battalion 3-16 were reorganized in Tegucigalpa in 1998, ostensibly as an anticrime measure. Summary executions by police and soldiers followed. Many victims were indigenous or labor-rights activists.

Poverty and crime remain huge concerns. Honduras has one of

★Negroponte went on to become George W. Bush's UN ambassador during the buildup to the Iraq invasion. During the occupation, he became Bush's ambassador to Iraq. He is now Deputy Secretary of State.

the worst murder rates on earth—twice as high as Colombia. Tourist warnings from various governments advise extreme caution around cities, rural areas, and much of the coastline. But other than *that* . . .

PANAMA

* United States v. Panama, variations on a theme

Panama is where Balboa reached the Pacific, waded into the water, and claimed the entire ocean for Spain. This would have been news to the Japanese. Balboa was later beheaded by his father-in-law, something every married man worries about at some point. Still, his discovery meant that the stuff Spain plundered from Peru could be sent by boat up to Panama, hoicked over the narrow bit, and then shipped home. Panama has been a 4-Way Stop between two continents and two oceans ever since.

After Spanish rule, Panama remained a part of Colombia for more than eighty years. A U.S. treaty with Colombia gave the U.S. exclusive rights to build railroads through Panama as of 1846, and Panama has remained under U.S. influence since. During a later Colombian civil war, President Teddy Roosevelt saw an opportunity to grab control of a potential canal, so the U.S. backed Panamanian independence. After this 1903 treaty—signed without any actual Colombians or Panamanians around—the Canal Zone became U.S. territory, and the rest of Panama functioned as a de facto U.S. colony for decades.

After WWII, the Canal Zone became home to both the U.S. Southern Command, which oversaw U.S. military and intelligence actions throughout Latin America, and the School of the Americas (SOA), a training facility to "promote democracy." Numerous SOA graduates became severe human-rights abusers, a situation the U.S. insists is a complete coincidence. Declassified training manuals indicate otherwise.

The U.S. also pushed for the creation of a U.S.-trained Panamanian army, which seized power in a 1968 coup run by Omar Torrijos, who went by the delightful title "Maximum Leader." Torrijos wasn't the Blofeld some of his contemporaries were, but he made more people disappear than David Copperfield. Torrijos also had better hair.

The U.S. presence was always a simmering insult to Panamanian pride, but relations became further complicated during the 1980s regime of Manuel "Pineapple Face" Noriega, the CIA's point man in Panama, who rose to power after Torrijos's plane somehow just blew up on its own. Afterward, nothing happened in Panama without Noriega's say-so; when one critic announced his opposition to Noriega, his head was found in a U.S. mail bag. Still, during the Reagan era, Noriega was a reliable U.S. asset, assisting U.S. operations in El Salvador, Honduras, and Nicaragua.

However, the cocaine boom in Colombia also turned Panama into a drug transshipment point and money laundry. As long as Noriega was a loyal Contra ally, the U.S. Drug Enforcement Agency praised his antinarcotics efforts. But once Noriega's cooperation was less than complete, he became an instant liability for his U.S. patrons. In 1988, Noriega was indicted in the United States for drug trafficking. His time was almost up.

After Noriega lost a 1989 election he tried to fix, he retained power only through repression. That December, President George H. W. Bush—the former CIA chief who had arranged Noriega's covert payments in the 1970s—ordered an invasion, claiming self-defense while stealth bombers attacked an army smaller than the NYPD. Hundreds and probably thousands of civilians died; tens of thousands were left homeless. In the invasion's first hours, the U.S. unilaterally swore in Panama's next president in the Canal Zone. So much for Panama's "independence."

Opinion throughout Latin America was strongly negative, and in the first years after the U.S. invasion, cocaine traffic doubled. So much for the anti-drug victory. At this writing, Pineapple Face is now in a Miami prison, where he is subject to only slightly more U.S. supervision than he was in Panama. Current U.S. parole policies would mandate Noriega's release about two weeks before this book's publication. Assuming his cell doesn't somehow just blow up on its own.

Panama's current president, Martín Torrijos, is the son of the nation's longtime dictator. The new Torrijos is a vocal supporter of Puerto Rican independence from the United States. I would not advise getting on any small planes with this man.

EUROPE

CHECHNYA

- Russia v. Chechen separatists allied with Dagestan Islamists

Russia says this war is over. The Chechens aren't quite convinced. And I could have started this chapter with those same words 148 years ago.

Chechnya has struggled with foreign invaders for at least five hundred years, battling Turks, Georgians, Cossacks, and finally Russians, who shoved their way in during the late 18th century, trying to secure Russia's borders with the Ottoman Empire (see "Turkey," p. 42).

In the 1830s, anti-Russian resistance united from Dagestan to roughly Ingushetia under a Sufi Muslim leader named Imam Shamil, but Shamil was captured by the Russians in 1859. The war was over. But also not.

After the Bolshevik Revolution, seven northern Caucasus regions—Chechnya, Abkhazia, Balkaria, Cherkessia, Dagestan, Kabarda, and Ossetia—proclaimed a North Caucasus Federation, but this was stomped by the Russians. All seven remain, with widely varying degrees of friction, inside Russia and Georgia to this day.

The Nazis crunched in during WWII, seeking Azerbaijan's oil. About 40,000 locals fought on Stalin's side. A few collaborated with the other bad guys, however, so in response, Stalin deported *everybody*—between 400,000 and 500,000 people—to Kazakhstan and Siberia. About half died on the way or in exile. Chechens were permitted to return home in 1957, but you can see why they'd be ticked for generations.

In 1990, a rebel All-National Congress of the Chechen People elected a former Soviet general, Dzhokhar Dudayev, as leader. (Dudayev had grown up in Kazakhstan after the forced deportations, so he was never exactly a Soviet team player.) In 1991, as other former Soviet republics stretched their legs, Dudayev and his men stormed the local government, declaring an independent Chechen republic. Their slogan, "Death or Freedom," still sounds creepy, but Patrick Henry once said something pretty similar.

However, virtually no government recognized their authority, and skilled non-Chechens left in droves, killing the economy and leading to a surge in crime. Anti-Dudayev Chechens called for Moscow's help, and in 1994 the Russians invaded. In 1995 Russia sealed off Grozny and bombed the crap out of it, killing perhaps 30,000 civilians, including ethnic Russians who got stuck with no place to run. After brutal urban warfare, the Russian army took what was left of the capital. Dudayev and pals went into guerrilla mode, assisted by Islamist fighters from across the region. For the Russian military, Chechnya became Afghanistan, Jr.

Fighters on both sides did horrible things. In 1995, Chechen guerrillas seized a hospital in Budennovsk, taking 1,500 hostages. After a standoff, the Chechens were allowed, in essence, to hit the Back button and go home. A similar crisis in Kizlyar was a further embarrassment to Moscow. Boris Yeltsin was starting to look like a weenie. A few months later, while struggling for reelection against a communist candidate, Yeltsin offered Dudayev a peace deal. Minutes after Dudayev picked up his satellite phone, his signal was traced and triangulated by spy satellites, and two laser-guided missiles blew Dudayev to bits. *Who's the weenie now!?* Yeltsin shouted. *Say hello to my little friend! Next time you're leading a rebel movement in the Caucasus, use text messaging.*

Three days before Yeltsin's second term began, the Chechens attacked Grozny under the new leadership of Shamil Basayev, named for Imam Shamil and the grandson of a fighter for the North Caucasus Federation. Despite being substantially outnumbered, Basayev's men retook Grozny, and the Russians offered a cease-fire, which held.

However, with no real infrastructure, one of Chechnya's main economic activities became kidnapping for ransom. Not the sort of thing to build a stable republic on. Perhaps no one thought of casinos.

Things soon worsified. After a minority Islamist movement rolled out of bed in Dagestan, Basayev and more than one thousand Islamist militants joined up to fight for an Islamic Republic of Dagestan. Russia responded with overwhelming force, fire-bombing Chechen fighters, Chechen training grounds, and anything that still smelled Chechen.

Almost immediately after the Chechen retreat, bombs went off in both Russia and Dagestan. Whoever was responsible, Moscow considered this pretext enough for another assault on Grozny. Russian rocket attacks killed hundreds of civilians, but the Russian army retook the city. (As to civilian casualties: given the Chechens' ties to foreign

Islamism, Russia simply whispers "Al-Qaeda" and the West usually shrugs.)

By February 2002, Vladimir Putin felt confident enough to describe the Chechen war as over, but Team Basayev began a series of truly horrific suicide attacks. The two most notorious: the 2002 taking of 850 hostages in a Moscow theater, leading to 129 deaths after the Russians responded with poison gas; and the 2004 kidnapping of 1,200 people at an elementary school in Beslan, leading to the deaths of 344.

Eventually, Basayev himself died in an explosion in Ingushetia. Chechen rebels say it was an accident, Russia says they got their man, and the autopsy says it was the work of rival Islamists. Whichever.

Grozny is now under reconstruction, but Chechnya is hardly quiet. Russia has installed a Chechen president, Ramzan Kadyrov, whose militia is widely alleged by human rights groups to have committed serious abuses; torture in Chechen prisons is said to be near universal. And at this writing, intermittent guerrilla actions continue in the Chechen highlands.

Maybe we should check back in another 148 years.

KOSOVO

- Albanian Muslim Kosovars v. Orthodox Serbs

Serbia considers Kosovo its historical heartland. Inconveniently, Serbs are outnumbered there ten to one.

Serbs and Albanians have crossed paths in Kosovo for a thousand years, but in the 1300s, Serbia ruled things from Belgrade all the way south into Greece. In this still-romanticized era, Kosovo was central to Serbian identity. But good times never last, and in 1389, the Ottomans chugged in (see "Turkey," p. 42), fought the Serbs in the Battle of Kosovo, and turned this Orthodox Christian heartland into a Muslim

185

domain. The loss still resonates in Serbian culture as a heroic, glorious defeat. If that seems perverse, remember the Alamo.

Ottoman rule over Serbia ended in 1878, and after WWI, Kosovo once again became part of the Kingdom of Serbia, which became part of the new federation of Yugoslavia in 1929. However, Kosovo's Albanian Muslim majority remains to this day.

WWII shredded Yugoslavia with the rest of Europe. Nazi influence extended over Croatia (which was particularly brutal to Serbs and other non-Croats) and Bosnia; Italy's sphere included Albania, Montenegro, and Kosovo. (By now, Albanians had also come to see Kosovo as Albanian. So that's two overlapping Greater Whatsits, Serbia and Albania, eyeballing the same land.) Anti-Nazi resistance came from Serbian militias ("Chetiniks") and Croatian partisans led by Josip Broz Tito; these two didn't get along, either.

After WWII, the Allies preferred Tito, who ruled a reunited Yugoslavia that sometimes opposed the Soviets almost as much as the West. Tito held the country's fractious factions—Catholic Croats and Slovenes, Orthodox Serbs, Muslim Bosniaks and Kosovars, and more—together by force, guile, mutual self-interest, and a general stomping of ethnicity. As a result, Belgrade again ruled Kosovo, and Albanian identity was temporarily squished.

In the 1960s, however, Belgrade loosened the screws slightly, and in 1974, Kosovars gained some constitutional autonomy, renewing a sense of identity. Later, as the Cold War ended, ethnic nationalism reemerged; Croatian and Bosnian declarations of independence led directly to major wars, as Serbs in each state fought to remain connected to Serbian rule, sometimes by getting rid of local non-Serbs.*

---

*A number of Croats, Bosniaks, and others were also found guilty of war crimes by the International Criminal Tribunal for the former Yugoslavia; atrocities were not only committed by one side. The vast majority of the convicted, however, were Serbs.

In Belgrade, Serbian president Slobodan Milosevic, who resembled the bastard child of Newt Gingrich and Eraserhead, had based much of his career on crude ethnic pride. After rolling back Kosovo's autonomy, Milosevic supported brutal Serbian militias in Croatia and Bosnia.

In 1995, the West brokered a series of accords in Dayton, Ohio, that helped stabilize things by creating two separate entities within Bosnia—a Serbian Republic (Republika Srpska, "RS" on the map) and a federation jointly run by Muslims and Croats. The deal has largely held. However, Dayton viewed Kosovo as a side issue, omitting it from the talks. This helped lead directly to more conflict.

Kosovo's independence movement had been led by the sharp-dressing Ibrahim Rugova, an advocate of democracy, peace, and snappy silk scarves. Rugova was twice elected Kosovo's president in unrecognized elections. Unfortunately, when Rugova couldn't gain a hearing in Dayton, more militant Kosovars gained credibility.

Cue the Kosovo Liberation Army (KLA), categorized by the U.S. envoy as "terrorists," at least before the U.S. intervened on their behalf. In 1998, the KLA began attacking policemen and other Serbian targets. Serbia responded by attacking civilian villages suspected of harboring KLA sympathizers. These massacres, in turn, convinced thousands of Albanians to join the KLA. On we go.

Militarily, the KLA were never particularly strong, but Milosevic's massive reaction would prove his undoing. In the summer of 1998, Serbs drove hundreds of thousands of Kosovars from their homes. At least two thousand people—possibly many more—were killed. After Serb atrocities in Bosnia and Croatia, the West had a short fuse, so in September 1998, NATO asked Milosevic to stop with the maiming, please.

In 1999, hostile negotiations were held at Rambouillet, France. After the UN's failures in Bosnia, the West insisted on a NATO presence not just in Kosovo, but all of Serbia. With Cold War tensions still fresh, Serbia said no dice. The result: eleven weeks of air strikes, characterized as "humanitarian bombing."

Before the first NATO bomb fell, Milosevic escalated aggression against the Kosovars, including mass evacuations and serious ethnic cleansing. NATO's aerial bombardment didn't stop the Kosovar-shoving. Roughly 200,000 Albanians fled during the 1998 conflict; 800,000 more were pushed off as NATO opened the bomb bay doors.

Speaking of which: "precision" NATO bombs struck not just Serbian military targets but also Kosovar refugee convoys, Albanian army positions, open-air markets, passenger trains and buses, KLA fighters, a prison, a hospital, the Chinese embassy, and even a house in Bulgaria. In the U.S., Native American groups noted the irony of fighting ethnic cleansing with "Apache" helicopters.

Come June, diplomats from Russia and Finland intervened, and Milosevic agreed to withdraw. The West proclaimed victory, although the final agreement is surprisingly similar to terms that might have been possible before the war. Kosovo was handed to the UN—not NATO, a key Rambouillet demand—and Kosovars began returning. Now the exodus began the other way: despite the KLA's dissolution, about 100,000 Serbs fled, fearing conflict and Albanian revenge. They weren't crazy; several KLA leaders are on trial in The Hague for war crimes against Serbs.

The UN has remained in charge of Kosovo ever since, pending some bright idea. Eight years later, there hasn't really been one.

Back in Belgrade, Milosevic banned observers from Serbia's 2000 elections, resulting in protests from Serbs themselves, building to a general strike and the public seizure of Serbia's parliament. In 2001, Serbia hauled Milosevic to jail, and in 2002 he went on trial in The Hague for crimes against humanity. Milosevic died before any verdict, but adding together Bosnia, Croatia, and Kosovo, the guy took at least 130,000 people with him.

In 2003, Yugoslavia ceased to exist, becoming the union of Serbia and Montenegro, which itself disintegrated when Montenegro de-Serbiated in 2006. In Kosovo, meanwhile, tensions remain high. In 2004, Kosovars attacked Serbians in Mitrovica and torched Serbian Orthodox churches. Serbs burned mosques in response.

In 2005, bombs exploded in Kosovo near the offices of the UN and the Organization of Security and Cooperation in Europe. In 2006, Serbian voters approved a new constitution declaring Kosovo an integral part of Serbia; Kosovars, naturally, boycotted the ballot. Five months later, the UN envoy unveiled a plan for Kosovo's independence; while Kosovars cheered, Serbs rejected it out of hand.

In early 2007, UN vehicles have been bombed by a self-proclaimed new KLA, and Kosovar protesters are marching again through Pristina. Back in Belgrade, Serbian nationalists retain a large slice of political power; their Radical party is now the largest in the Serbian parliament.

Fortunately, major war seems unlikely anytime soon.

Unfortunately, so does major peace.

UNITED KINGDOM

- "War on terror" and domestic reactions
- Fragile but growing peace in Northern Ireland
- Variable minor frictions elsewhere

The United Kingdom of Great Britain & Northern Ireland
plus a few dozen warmer islands
and a nice bit of Spain, thank you

North Sea

Atlantic Ocean

Scotland

Edinburgh

⚑ Catholics

✠ Protestants

〰 Muslims added for extra flavor

Belfast N. I.

Dublin

Ireland

Liverpool

Wales

Leeds

Manchester

Birmingham

London

England

Gibraltar, Bermuda, Anguilla, the Caymans, and assorted warmer bits

English Channel

France

Prepare to be confused. The UK is a union of four countries—England, Scotland, Wales, and Northern Ireland—three of whom are the largest remnants of a once-global empire. But 80 percent of the population lives in England, so people often confuse "England" with "UK," which it isn't.

"Great Britain" isn't the UK, either; it's the island where England is. The "British Isles" would be Great Britain plus Ireland, except the phrase annoys Ireland, which isn't British. But a "Briton" is from anywhere in the UK, including Northern Ireland. Which, if you look at a map, doesn't include the northernmost part of Ireland. And when a British person says "Europe," they mean Europe except for the UK, even though the UK is part of Europe.

This may be why Australians use the word *Poms* for all involved, saving extra mental energy for drinking. No one knows where the word *Poms* comes from, either.

WALES

Wales was annexed by Henry VIII five hundred years ago and has been England's picked-on kid brother ever since.

Welsh nationalism only got serious in 1965, when England decided to bring water to Liverpool by flooding an entire Welsh village, and Wales realized they couldn't do squat about it. Up rose a nationalist party called the Plaid Cymru, which involves nothing plaid. Incomprehensibility has been Wales's main weapon ever since. (*Cymru* means "Wales," and you are about to mispronounce it badly. Really. The Welsh alphabet doesn't care what you think. Take your best shot.)

The Welsh nationalist symbol is the leek, a kind of large green onion. No one knows why. Supposedly, Welsh archers were told to take a leek before the battle of Agincourt, the Welsh charged into combat with large green onions on their heads, and Welshmen have been taking leeks wherever they go ever since. (On the other hand, England's national symbol is a lion, despite the complete lack of native cats of any kind. As I said, England is confusing. And by "England," I mean "the UK." Shit.)

In 1998, Wales got a national assembly, but London still calls the shots. So far, the assembly's big accomplishment has been creating a special commission to decide how many more decisions they should ever make. (Honest.)

Cymru, finally, is pronounced "Kum-ree." Told you. The Welsh name for the UK is *Teyrnas Unedig Prydain Fawr a Gogledd Iwerddon.* You can pronounce this correctly by gargling a Styrofoam ball while hitting your neck with a mallet.

SCOTLAND

Scotland is a fictional country invented in 1822 by novelist Sir Walter Scott to impress King George IV. In this mythical land, ancient clans wear kilts decorated with tartans, wee lassies dance highland flings, and people listen to bagpipes intentionally. In no way should this be confused with the real country of the same name.

The royal motto of Scotland is *Nemo Me Impune Lacessit,* Latin for "Nobody provokes me with impunity." That's the *national motto.* Do not piss off Scottish people. They will cut you. Not because of hate. As a matter of national pride.

Until visiting Scotland, I'd never heard the phrase "Knife Crime" in my life. But "Knife Crime" is its *own separate category* there. In Glasgow, five minutes after I get out of the car, there's a giant electronic billboard imploring me to help fight this "Knife Crime." Atop the Glasgow Royal Concert Hall.

Classy joint.

I repeat: do *not* provoke the Scottish. You will not have impunity.

Unlike Wales, Scotland has a new parliament with a hint of actual power, and its largest party is keen on full independence. Its most notable act of rebellion so far, however: spending $800 million on a new parliament building for themselves.

They didn't even use a knife to do it.

NORTHERN IRELAND

Catholic Ireland was ruled by the Protestant UK until 1921, when the original Irish Republican Army (IRA) began guerrilla raids, assassinations, and attacks on police. The UK responded with horrible violence, galvanizing the Irish rebellion. Shortly before the IRA was about to begin attacks within England proper, London made peace with what would now be called terrorists, granting home rule to twenty-six of Ireland's thirty-two counties.

However, six northeastern counties had Protestant majorities; the deal allowed these counties to choose to remain in the UK. The North soon descended into civil war between "Nationalists" (favoring an Irish nation, not a British one) against "Unionists" (wishing union with the UK, not Ireland); choosing the right synonym was key. Meanwhile, in the South, Irish factions favoring and opposing the treaty engaged in their *own* civil war. As someone from an Irish-American family, I find this plausible.

Never mind that the religious differences were minor, arising only because Henry VIII got sick of his first wife. And both sides were avowed social conservatives: Nationalists were strict followers of Rome, while the Unionists went even further, including a memorable "Save Ulster from Sodomy" campaign in 1977.

The South pulled things together, but in the North, another generation of Republicans took up the fight against Unionists and the British. Hatred being its own seed, these Troubles lasted until 1998, when everyone decided on—wait for it—a majority vote.

Despite a few bumps in the road—like an IRA splinter faction continuing occasional fire-bomb attacks—something like peace is at hand. A new power-sharing joint government is in place, and in Belfast, visitors can even take a "Troubles Tour," a guided bus ride through scenes of violence and horror, before settling over a latte at Starbucks. The increasing calm is reinforced by a growing economy, gradual integration with the rest of Europe, and increasing immigration.

At the last census, about 10 percent of Northern Ireland wasn't born in Northern Ireland; soon, neither Catholics nor Protestants will comprise a majority. Many new citizens don't care if their bread transsubstantiates or consubstantiates, as long as they get something to eat. So ultimately, Northern Ireland no longer looks quite like Northern Ireland in part *because* it doesn't look like Northern Ireland.

ENGLAND

Despite the 1998 Good Friday Agreement, Irish militants have set off several explosions in London, which has also been targeted repeatedly by Islamist extremists; the latter are by far the graver concern.

In 2005, three subway trains and a bus were bombed by four Al-Qaeda sympathizers, killing fifty-two people and injuring more than seven hundred. It was the worst bombing in London since WWII. The attackers, however, were barely known to British intelligence; they may simply have been disaffected extremists acting without the direct knowledge of Al-Qaeda's Big Bad. Until the big picture is clearer, similar attacks might be severely challenging to prevent.

In March 2007, three men from Leeds were arrested for conspiring with the subway bombers, and in April, five other Britons were convicted of conspiracy to detonate an Oklahoma City–style fertilizer bomb. Their ringleader had met with two of the subway bombers. Small world? Hardly. British police are reportedly monitoring two thousand suspected Al-Qaeda supporters.

"Suspected," unfortunately, has become the operative word. Since 9-11, the UK has attempted to defend democracy and freedom by radically expanding the surveillance of its private citizens. According to the BBC, the UK now has 4.2 million security cameras, and London has become one of the most heavily surveilled places on earth. A typical resident will appear on surveillance camera as many as three hundred times each day.

The UK has also passed antiterrorism laws that potentially erode human rights. As in the United States, UK law now allows the government to detain terror suspects indefinitely, facing accusations they are never told; to seize their property; and to inflict cruel and unusual prison conditions—all before trial. Many such measures apply not just to immigrants, but potentially to any UK citizen, including "control orders" amounting to perpetual house arrest without trial. Unfortunately, draconian measures didn't stop the subway bombing, which was apparently a complete surprise, nor a similar attempt two weeks later that failed only because the explosive charges failed to detonate.

Obviously, only a tiny minority of British Muslims condoned the London attacks; most found them as abhorrent as anyone else. But that didn't stop Britons from vandalizing mosques in London, Bristol, Leeds, and a dozen other locations. The circle turns.

It's ironic that the UK's most serious threats are exacerbated by religion, given that Great Britain is one of the more secular places on earth. In the 2001 national census, nearly 1 percent of respondents jokingly gave their religion as "Jedi." The UK even puts Charles Darwin on the £10 note, something their conservative U.S. allies should never find out.

Elsewhere, the UK has had three "Cod Wars" with Iceland over fishing rights, involving net-cutting, territorial line-crossing, and (I like to imagine) ship-to-ship chum fights using catapults. Since both countries are overfishing, this will sadly be a short-term problem.

In 1982, Argentina invaded Britain's nearby outpost in the Falkland Islands, which are so remote that fishermen sometimes resort to live penguins as a source of cooking fuel. (Actually true.) The shaky Argentine junta seized the islands hoping that a cheap military stunt would swell national pride, never suspecting that Margaret Thatcher's own then-shaky government would see a similar stunt as an issue of survival, soon sending British troops halfway around the earth just to keep the penguins on the fire. Nine hundred dead soldiers later, Thatcher's "Operation Corporate" (irony unintended) was victorious, and the Union Jack again flew proudly over the middle of nowhere.

In 2007, protesters in Buenos Aires burned British flags on the twenty-fifth anniversary. News reports are unclear as to whether penguins were involved.

SPAIN

- Islamist bombing, 2004
- Basque and Catalan separatist movements
- Minor friction over Gibraltar, Ceuta, and Melilla

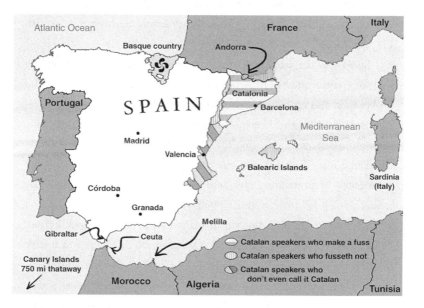

ro-Magnons first flooded Spain 35,000 years ago, and northern European vacationers make one wonder if the flow ever really ended. Next came Goths, Visigoths (Goths wearing goggles), Celts, Greeks, Phoenicians, Carthaginians, and finally Arabic-speaking Moors, who made the area a Muslim stronghold for half a millennium. The Moors also pushed north into France, where the foreigners were met with hostility. Imagine that.

The Moorish capital at Córdoba (home of rich Corinthian leather) became the most advanced city on earth—simply *the* place to be in the

9th century. However, the Moors' last stronghold at Granada fell in 1492, and the region became home to a variety of kingdoms speaking separate languages, several of which survive today.

No one expected the Spanish Inquisition, but it began partly out of fear of Muslim attacks. (It was, in a sense, the Guantánamo of its day.) Christian kingdoms continued to consolidate via royal marriages and/or mass killings, and by the early sixteenth century, the Spanish Empire was on.

Spain was the world's leading power for about 150 years, ruling most of Central and South America, islands from the Caribbean to the Philippines, and chunks of central Europe. The Spanish throne, however, was held by the Hapsburg family, who consolidated their rule through intermarriage, lusting for power and each other in apparently equal amounts. With a family tree resembling bamboo, royalty became identifiable by protruding jaws and slobbering tongues. In short, the reign in Spain fell mainly to the plain.

Ultimately, in 1665 the world's first global empire was inherited by a drooling ninny, Charles II, who was so inbred that he was unable to chew without help. Fortunately, both Charles's mother and his father's niece were always on hand; they were the *exact same person.* Charles was so inbred that he descended from one great-great-great-grandmother ("Joanna the Mad") in exactly fourteen* different ways.

Charles's favorite hobby, incidentally, was shooting very large guns.

Fortunately for the gene pool, this DNA Plinko game came to a halt when Charles proved incapable of reproduction. His heirless death was followed by the War of Spanish Succession, which is a more polite name than the War of the Impotent Moron. Ten years and 1.2 million deaths later, Spain had lost most of its European claims, including

---

*A Hapsburg genealogy diagram and some colored pencils—rainy-day fun!

Gibraltar. After that, Spain had its Bourbon period, which was understandable.

The Napoleonic years brought more violence, weakening the Empire further. Colonies declared independence, and in 1898, the U.S. blamed Spain for a questionable explosion ("Remember the *Maine!*"), seizing the few overseas possessions Spain had left (see "The Philippines," p. 143).

Dictatorship was followed by the revolutionary Spanish Republic, an idealistic attempt at anarchism (or democracy, or socialism, or communism, depending which heavily armed idealist you asked). Somehow, the anarchists never got organized. Instead, fascists armed by Mussolini and the Nazis won the Spanish Civil War, whose atrocities inspired Picasso, Orwell, and Hemingway. As unspeakable tragedies go, it was an artistic success.

Generalissimo Francisco Franco's fascist regime ruled with an iron grip until 1975, when his persistent death brought *Saturday Night Live* into power in the U.S. However, Franco's intended successor had been killed by a car bomb planted by Basque separatists. As a replacement dictator, Franco designated Juan Carlos I, a descendant of every blueblood from Queen Victoria to Burger King. Surprisingly, however, Juan Carlos became a freedom-loving moderate whose reign has been all about establishing a lasting republic. He immediately sought democratic reforms, relinquishing absolute power in 1978. Juan Carlos now seems content to yacht around with his Greek wife, cut ceremonial ribbons, and occasionally shoot a very large gun.

Ironically, Spain might still be a dictatorship but for a terrorist act meant to destabilize everything. So you never know.

Basques, whose odd language and egalitarian culture developed separately from the rest of Spain, are themselves split over independence. However, the separatist ETA (*Euskadi Ta Askatasuna,* Basque for "Estimated Time of Arrival") has killed about a thousand people since

1959. ETA had some public support during the Franco years, but the growth of democracy deglamorized random carnage. (It doesn't help that the Basque logo looks like a swastika made from swirling blood drops.) Post–9-11 security has also cramped ETA's style, but despite promising a permanent cease-fire, ETA just blew up a parking garage at the Madrid airport. Odd definition of "permanent."

The Catalonian independence movement presents little violence hazard, since Catalonia is already the richest part of Spain, the Catalan language is related to Spanish, the two peoples have been joined at the hip for five hundred years, and their economies are utterly intertwined. On a lark, I once even joined a march in Barcelona, learning slogans phonetically and repeating them for TV cameras. It was safe and fun and there were pretty girls. My kind of protest.

Although Franco oppressed Catalonia plenty, Catalonians are now recognized as a distinct nationality by the Spanish constitution. Only about one in three would rattle for full independence. Still, a vocal minority hollers about unifying the "Catalan countries," including bits of France and Italy and a stretch of Valencia where Valencians prefer to call the language Valencian. So this movement for linguistic identity can't even agree on what the language is called. Nice.

Catalan is also spoken in Andorra, a Pyrenees tax haven whose entire population would fit inside Giants Stadium. There are cows on the coat of arms. This concludes Andorra.

To the south, Spain periodically decides they'd like Gibraltar back from the UK, citing "territorial integrity." Never mind that virtually no Gibraltans want union with Spain, so Madrid's best case is a hostile mess they can't win. In 2006, Spain agreed to chill.

Besides, Spain still maintains two enclaves, Ceuta and Melilla, on the Moroccan coast. Morocco cites "territorial integrity," too, possibly just to annoy Spain. Of greater concern is the immigration issue created by two European Union outposts dropped onto a continent where desperation is a main export. Surveillance cameras, razor wire, and tear gas have followed.

Unfortunately, so has Islamist extremism. In 2003, the conservative government of José María Aznar supported the Iraq invasion, despite overwhelming public opposition. Then on March 11, 2004, just days before national elections, bombs exploded on Madrid commuter trains, killing almost two hundred and wounding over two thousand. Most of the culprits were Moroccans sympathetic to Al-Qaeda.

The Aznar government, however, pushed blame onto ETA, a move widely seen as an attempt to delay discussion of how Aznar's Iraq policy may have led to retaliation. Feeling doubly betrayed, Spaniards voted Aznar out of office. Aznar's successor eventually pulled out of Iraq while increasing the number of troops sent to Afghanistan. This was often oversimplified in the U.S. media as "giving in to terrorists." Spain's government has been derided by U.S. conservatives ever since.

GERMANY

- Peaceful republic with no external enemies
- Pretty weird, given its history
- Growing extremism in the east, more like the Germany we expect

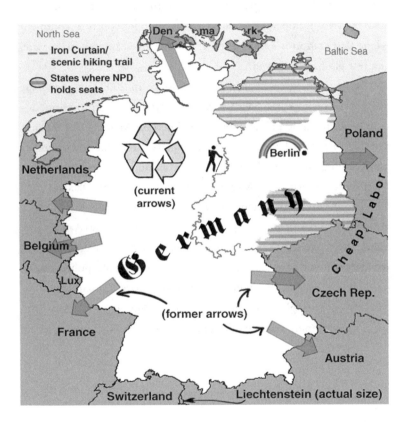

In the last hundred years, Germany has called itself an Empire, a Reich, and a Republic. Two world wars later, *Republic* seems like the way to go.

Germany's distant predecessor, the Holy Roman Empire, was founded by Charlemagne on December 25, 800, despite the holiday weekend. This "First Reich" ruled most of central Europe before splintering along religious lines. (In Bohemia, Protestants tried to execute their Catholic oppressors by flinging them from a high window. Fortunately, the prisoners landed in a mound of horse poop and survived. Five hundred years later, that's all most people remember. Worth considering, next time you're about to start a war.)

Napoleon's rumbles further delayed nation-state-itude, but in 1862, Prussia finally got a quality quarterback in Otto von Bismarck, a master statesman devoted to unifying Germany. After alliance-building and a few carefully chosen wars, boom: a "Second Reich," encompassing all German-speaking lands but Austria. This lasted until WWI.

After the Germans lost this particular War to End All Wars (collect 'em all!), the succeeding republic might have worked, but for the collapse of every aspect of society. Reparations owed to the Allies were economically crippling. Left-wing strikes and right-wing violence crushed any hope of manufacturing much. Eventually, Germany paid off its debts by inflating its own currency, wiping out the savings of nearly every German. By the 1930s, the economy was shredded, political murders were common, and extremists of all stripes had armed militias.

Enter Adolf Hitler, whose speeches often recited worst-case scenarios, promoting himself as the homeland's only protector. Elections in 1932 gave the Nazis one-third of the Reichstag, enough to paralyze the government completely, creating further tension. Finally, on January 29, 1933, Hitler was appointed chancellor by President Paul von Hindenburg, who later exploded in a massive fireball while docking in Lakehurst, New Jersey. Despite only minority support, Hitler consolidated power largely through legal means. In the panic following the Reichstag fire (responsibility for which is still controversial), the Nazis rammed through laws giving Hitler the right to suspend habeas corpus and interpret the constitution at whim.

Tens of millions of corpses later, the Russians had repelled the Nazis at Stalingrad, the Allies had landed at Normandy, and Hitler had shot himself in his bunker. The History Channel has been in English ever since.

The West and the Soviets divvied up the place, splitting Germany between communist East and capitalist West. In the West, the U.S. Marshall Plan poured billions into rebuilding. In the East, the secret police collected cotton swabs that had been rubbed against the groins of dissidents, so their personal odors might be pursued by dogs. You can guess who won the hearts and minds.

About 2.5 million East Germans—one in ten—fled west until 1961, when the damn commies built the Berlin Wall (aka the "Anti-Fascist Protection Rampart"), imprisoning their own citizens. But in 1989, neighboring countries took down many border restrictions, thousands of East Germans took the chance to flee, those left behind

East meets West.

took down the wall itself, and the U.S. right wing took credit at every opportunity.

Unfortunately, the sudden assimilation of 17 million people—many poor, housed in crumbling cities, and culturally estranged—ain't easy. (Imagine the U.S. suddenly declaring Mexico the 51st state; this over-states the case wildly, but it's a fun start.) The once-booming West now had to carry the developing East.

Despite over $100 billion in total subsidies, unemployment in the East still hovers around 20 percent. The problem may be structural: Eastern consumers prefer Western products, but Western businesses don't hire from the East, finding even cheaper labor *farther* east—in Poland and the Czech Republic. Meanwhile, young Easterners go west at first chance, draining talent and energy. Triple whammy. So Easterners often feel colonized or abandoned, while some Westerners blame "backwards" Easterners. Ironically, Slavs to the east who threw off the Soviets have now become labor for Germans.

During a 1960s need for such labor, West Germany created a large guest-worker program, but the Iron Curtain forced the government to look farther south—to Turkey. Many Turks settled and built families, giving Germany one of the largest Muslim populations in Europe. German society now struggles with a bit of cultural angst.

Unfortunately, that tension also fuels neo-Nazism in two ways: where the presence of Turkish families doesn't stimulate a general xenophobia, their frequently anti-Israeli views contribute to lingering anti-Semitism. Despite generations vowing to "never forget," a disturbing 2001 survey by the Forsa Institute (Berlin's answer to the Gallup Poll) found that about half of East Germans between fourteen and twenty-five—and 62 percent of East German high school students—thought the Nazi regime "had its good side."

German intelligence tracks more than 150 right-wing extremist groups with 40,000 total supporters; maybe 4,000 are hardcore. Most are in the East, where anti-Semitic hate crimes occur four times more frequently per capita than in the West. The National Democratic Party (NPD), the neo-Nazi party of choice, has recently won assembly seats in two states. Not surprisingly, Israel's ambassador recently stated that Jews here "do not feel safe."

Of course, the vast majority of Germans abhor such extremists; in fact, Germany has become stunningly liberal, with most of today's Germans far more likely to light up a joint than a Reichstag. Anyone reading this book who despairs to think the world can't change need only look at Germany, whose recent generations have tended to utterly abhor the Nazi past. There's even an interesting lesson here: old Nazis themselves generally didn't change. But the next generation of Germans were completely different. That may be how the world changes, too—not within individuals, but with new generations. This seems equally apparent in Northern Ireland, South Africa, and other countries whose pasts have been disappearing of late.

In any case, whatever the reason, the great-grandchildren of Nazis now take to the streets to *protest* war, the Iron Curtain itself is becoming a scenic hiking trail, and Berlin proudly hosts the annual rainbow-friendly "Love Parade."

Still, you can tell it's Germany: even in expressing love, joy, and hope, there has to be marching involved.

BONUS STRESS:
HOW TO START A WAR IN 10 EASY STEPS

1. Find something you want on somebody else's soil. This can be anything: natural resources, access to sea routes, living space in the east, the hometown of your deity, or a personal sense of vindication. Use your imagination! There are no wrong answers.

2. Begin convincing your public that you desire only peace. If this isn't credible because your country fights a lot of wars, convince your public that you are only concerned for their safety. If this isn't credible because you've gotten a lot of them killed, tell them you're talking to God.

3. If you run a dictatorship, buy/bribe/imprison/kill your country's media so your message will not be contradicted. Proceed to Step 4. If you do not run a dictatorship, simply repeat your messages, constantly, every single day. Exaggerate and contradict yourself as necessary. The media will dutifully recite each claim, no matter how outrageous, as part of each day's news. Even a scientific debunking cannot hurt your message; this will play simply as controversy. Finally, deny further access to any media outlets that do not faithfully repeat your claims. They must eventually cooperate merely to stay in business.

4. Demonize the country you want to attack. If your citizens are sophisticated enough not to fear millions of strangers who have done them no harm, simply demonize the leader of your target nation. This figure will soon appear to be synonymous with the entire population. (This will also help train your citizens to become receptive to *you* as synonymous with *them;* see Step 5.) In any case, make the other side appear as subhuman as possible. If their government or army has ever committed a war crime—and most have—point this out constantly. Use visual aids.

5. Make yourself personally synonymous with the national welfare. Pose with flags. Use the word *strong* a lot when talking about yourself. Stand in front of a mass of soldiers. However, do not wear the uniform; you lead the *nation,* not just the military. (At best, you will look like another general, inviting rivals; at worst, you will look ridiculous.)

6. (a) Question the patriotism, honesty, and/or religious virtue of anyone who disagrees with you. Imply that they are traitors. Meanwhile, reward the inevitable toadies in politics and the press who insist on the truth of even your contradictory claims. Let them be seen in your presence; they will become overwhelmed with loyalty. (b) Imprison people; it doesn't matter who. Imprisoning people shows how important your goal is, while both intimidating your opponents and impressing your toadies. If possible, imprison members of the target nation *and* domestic dissidents, implying their equivalence.

7. Nurture fear and a sense of righteous persecution. No public supports a war if they consider themselves the unjust aggres-

sors. Most human beings are basically decent. *You must not let this influence their decision-making process.* Convince your public that the *other* side is hell-bent on war and that they cannot be placated. Therefore, *your* war will be moral because it is self-defense. To your toadies, their self-defense will logically extend to attacking your domestic opponents, reinforcing the power of Step 6.

8. When peace overtures are made, denounce them as exactly the sort of thing your devious opponents would do to buy time/weaken your resolve/trick you into an unfair deal. Make it clear that by offering peace, your opponents are giving you no option but to attack. In self-defense.

9. Attack. In self-defense. The precise moment of invasion should be dictated by the start of TV prime time in your home country. Simply count the number of time zones from your target to your TV studios and adjust accordingly. Don't worry if this means you're attacking at 3 A.M.; explosions and tracer bullets look brighter on night shoots anyway.

10. Repeat all of the above as needed until either (a) you get everything, (b) you can plausibly *claim* you got everything, (c) a bloody stalemate develops that even *you* realize will eventually weaken your rule, or (d) your head is put on a pike by angry subjects and your corpse is ripped to shreds in anger. If you have heirs who may someday assume your mantle, teach them how to play, too, so your victory/frustration/humiliating losses/erasure from history can be celebrated/avenged/avenged/avenged. *Have fun!*

BONUS BONUS STRESS:
AN EXPERT SPEAKS

Why, of course, the *people* don't want war. . . . Why would some poor slob on a farm want to risk his life in a war when the best that he can get out of it is to come back to his farm in one piece. . . . But, after all, it is the *leaders* of the country who determine the policy and it is always a simple matter to drag the people along, whether it is a democracy or a fascist dictatorship or a Parliament or a Communist dictatorship . . . the people can always be brought to the bidding of the leaders. That is easy. All you have to do is tell them they are being attacked and denounce the pacifists for lack of patriotism and exposing the country to danger. It works the same way in any country.

—Nazi Luftwaffe commander Hermann Göring, interviewed by psychologist Gustave Gilbert, during his trial for crimes against humanity, 1946

CONCLUSION

The world can certainly seem like a ridiculously hostile place. While writing this, I've sometimes needed to watch the Three Stooges for ten-minute bursts, just to stay sane. And even that involves brothers slapping each other.

When this project began, I thought patterns might emerge from the *types* of violence:

Friendly graffiti in Greece.

maybe religious wars outlast economic ones, maybe ethnicity or poverty are key, or maybe one ideology just produces lots of jerks. Patterns *do* exist, it turns out, but not where I thought.

Fear seems the biggest constant; a stunning number of aggressive acts—even Hitler's annexation of the Sudetenland—have been rationalized as noble self-defense. And of course the world *is* scary; we *do* all die someday. So people buy it when you tell them to fear each other.

Ego is an enormous obvious factor, too: a sense of cultural superiority helps enable us to see other people as less than human. Ideological, irrational certainty about being right or (in the worst case) entitled by a god is particularly hazardous. Paradoxically, it's precisely when we think we're most justified that we're capable of the greatest harm.

Of course, fear, pride, certitude, and the inability to see others as equally human are things many of us experience in youth (and with luck, grow out of). Sure enough, German researcher Gunnar Heinsohn has found an extremely strong link between a society's youthfulness and its likelihood of conflict. When a third of the population is under twenty-nine, brace for trouble; the more people under fifteen, the more likely you are to have a war. Not coincidentally, a disproportionate amount of violent crime is also committed by males eighteen to twenty-four—almost exactly the same age group and gender that most armies find ideal. So *of course* armies recruit young men to engage in organized violence.

Venezuelan murderer and criminal-of-all-trades Carlos the Jackal: pop street icon.

Speaking as a former young male, this makes sense. When you have the body of an adult, the mind of a child, no idea where you're going, and a desperate desire to find out, any alpha male can be made to seem pretty cool.

I also imagined that religious, ethnic, and economic wars might carry distinct characters. Instead, it seems that extremism on one side simply breeds extremism on the other, of whatever variety has already taken root. Economic anger in one direction may inflame racial hatred in the other, or a land grab may magnify religious hatred. And of course motivations can overlap. Mix and match. And once any war starts, there's often a familiar descent into self-perpetuating chaos, criminality, they-started-its, and further extremism. The original causes may not even matter eventually.

I'm most surprised to find that rigid ideology of any kind—religious, economic, you name it—seems so dangerous. Maybe that's the spark needed to overcome reason. Want to establish a Christian nation? Muslim? Buddhist? This small book—an incomplete, half-competent glimpse at just one instant of history—has examples of each gone haywire. Claiming to speak with any deity seems like a pretty good disqualification from positions of power. But it's not just religion. Want to insist on communism? Socialism? Capitalism? Self-reliance? A nation, an ethnicity, a piece of land, a language? Any of these, dictated, is making a mess somewhere right this second.

Over and over, carnage follows whenever somebody decides that their answer—colonizing others, crushing all socialists or capitalists, wiping out that bothersome ethnicity, executing the infidels, whatever—is the only right answer.

I'm tempted to wonder if the innate human desire for simple, universal answers *is* the problem. It's a powerful impulse; when harnessed by the scientific method (a system of perpetual doubt and requestioning, remember), this yearning has spectacularly expanded our understanding of ourselves and the entire world. But when left unbridled, lacking critical feedback—"checks and balances," in political terms—the same impulse may lead us to simply choose whatever answer we like. This can be breathtakingly destructive, almost anywhere we look.

And once we choose any answer, our egos seem to get attached, even in the face of overwhelming evidence. Our beliefs feel almost like part of our bodies (which, on a neurological level, they *are*), so intellectually defending a favorite idea becomes confused with physical self-defense. Which is insane. Common sense tells us that there probably isn't one religious, political, economic, or social system that is best for everyone, everywhere. You wouldn't run a desert island the way you'd run Wall Street. You wouldn't run a plane in an emergency the way you'd run a school board. We don't even rely on one set of rules in a single day, adapting to different cultural norms in work, family, sports, church, and so on. That's just in one day of one ordinary life in one place.

There are six billion people in our family, in 192 different countries, worshipping hundreds of gods and speaking thousands of different languages. Misunderstandings and conflict are part of human existence. Among our own, however we define that, all humankind is capable of amazing good. But confuse or frighten us, and all hell breaks loose.

We, humankind, *are* all One. But that One can be a total jerk sometimes.

Retreating from all this would be perfectly sane, by the way. Sit and stare for a while if you feel the need.

But isolation is also part of the problem. It's a lot easier to become fanatic about one idea when you're not exposed constantly to lots of others. Almost every despot in these pages tries to control the media, cut off the flow of ideas, and make people unaware of the influences of other cultures all over the world. So stepping away isn't the answer.

Instead, maybe it's all a matter of getting a better perspective. For all the war stuff we've been looking at, how much of the world is actually at relative peace, at least at the moment? Believe it or not . . . almost all of it.

North America, a bloody mess for most of the 19th century? Not one active war. Central America, a slaughterhouse twenty years ago? The West Indies? The South Pacific? All are comparatively calm. South America? Even Colombia may be settling down. Much of Europe was an abattoir in the 20th century. Not anymore. Southeast Asia, where uncounted millions so recently died? Overall, things are improving.

Get an atlas and cross off the countries that you'd *really* never visit any part of because you know that they're just too dangerous. There may be dozens, but even then, you'll

Vaclav Havel's Prague prison cell; once he was president, the prison became a hotel where you newly appreciate freedom.

be surprised at how little you trim. Every city has its bad neighborhoods; that doesn't mean you can't love living there. Same with Earth: except for some specific dicey bits, most of our planet is still full of wonderful surprises.

In Singapore, the rare authoritarian slogan that can help you smile on a bad day.

Leaders everywhere still make terrible mistakes all the time, and that sucks. But our leaders now usually make much *better* mistakes than the leaders who came before, almost everywhere you look.

Just 150 years ago, the United States still practiced slavery, colonialism was considered the natural order, and every major power in Europe simply assumed they had the right to carve up the world. Just a hundred years ago, women couldn't vote, almost anywhere on the planet. In 1950, there was no such thing as a computer for sale. Just twenty-five years ago, who would have imagined that the Soviet Union was about to collapse, China would embrace capitalism, or that Nelson Mandela would become the face of South Africa?

A giggling kid startles me by doing a perfectly timed running flip in front of my lens, Muizenberg, South Africa.

It's not certain we'll figure things out. But how can we possibly despair?

After thousands of years of struggling in isolation, humankind is learning and connecting incredibly quickly, and at an accelerating pace. It's hard to imagine now, but when I was a young man, it was almost impossible to consider and interact with numerous different cultures, thousands of miles away, all over the world.

Penang

For many of today's young people—the folks who will very soon decide whether to commit pointless mass violence or become tomorrow's international leaders—it's becoming almost impossible *not* to.

There is tremendous joy in that thought.

Cairo

There is hope.

And best of all . . . you're *it*.

Tobago

Don't hate anybody. Ever.

And you'll know at least that much is possible.